NO DOUBT

MASTERING THE POWER OF BELIEF

NO DOUBT

MASTERING THE POWER OF BELIEF

EMBRACE CERTAINTY
IGNITE TRANSFORMATION

By David Byars

ARPress
ILLUMINATING IDEAS.
EMPOWERING VOICES

ARPress
45 Dan Road Suite 5
Canton MA 02021

Hotline: 1(888) 821-0229
Fax: 1(508) 545-7580

Ordering Information:

Quantity sales. Special discounts are available on quantity purchases by corporations, associations, and others. For details, contact the publisher at the address above.

Printed in the United States of America.

ISBN-13:   Paperback   979-8-89330-226-4
                eBook   979-8-89330-225-7
                Hardcover   979-8-89330-227-1

Library of Congress Control Number: 2024900601

DEDICATION

I dedicate this book to my baby brother, Benjamin Coleman Byars, whose unwavering will and determination serve as a beacon of inspiration to rise to greater heights and master the challenges that life presents. May the pages of this book reflect the same spirit of resilience, curiosity, and courage that you embody, guiding you on your own journey of mastering the power of belief. Your boundless enthusiasm and potential remind us all that with belief, there are no limits to what we can achieve.

EPIGRAPH

Therefore,

I tell you,

whatever you ask for in prayer,

believe that you have received it,

and it will be yours.

(Mark 11:24 NIV)

Table Of Contents

PART II
INTRODUCTION
CHAPTER 16
CHAPTER 17
CHAPTER 18
CHAPTER 19
CHAPTER 20
CHAPTER 21
CHAPTER 22
CHAPTER 23
CHAPTER 24
CHAPTER 25
CHAPTER 26
CHAPTER 27
CHAPTER 28
CHAPTER 29
CHAPTER 30
CHAPTER 31

Foreword

In a world teeming with complexities and uncertainties, belief emerges as a force that weaves the tapestry of human existence. It is both a driving force and a guiding compass, shaping the course of history and defining the contours of our individual lives. As my dear friend Dr. Davis Byars has embarked on this compelling journey, by writing this powerful book, in the pages of "Mastering the Power of Belief," we find ourselves standing at the crossroads of understanding, curiosity, and introspection.

In these times of transformation and upheaval, the significance of belief cannot be overstated. It influences not only the decisions we make but also the values we uphold, the dreams we pursue, and the relationships we forge. It is the bedrock upon which societies are built, cultures flourish, and civilizations evolve. It is the source of both solace and strife, hope and despair, inspiration and destruction.

As we traverse the chapters that delve into the multifaceted nature of belief, we encounter its myriad expressions and the diverse pathways through which it takes root in the human psyche. He explores the wellsprings of belief, be it in the realm of religion and spirituality or grounded in scientific inquiry. He confronts the power of authority figures to shape our convictions and the ways in which societal norms influence our collective consciousness.

He confronts the paradox of belief as a coping mechanism during adversity, offering solace and comfort in the face of uncertainty, while at the same time, acknowledging its potential to obscure reality and hinder progress. Through the lens of belief, he peers into the influence of media and information in shaping collective narratives and shaping the trajectory of nations.

Dr. Davis Byars shows us how this exploration would be incomplete without confronting the dark underbelly of belief, where its power has been wielded to sow discord, suppress voices, and perpetuate injustice. He grapples with the implications when belief is polarized, leading to a divided society where truth becomes subjective and objective standards erode.

Yet, as we journey through these complexities, we also find hope and possibility. The power of belief, when harnessed for collective good, can inspire visionary leaders to bring about profound change, dismantle oppressive systems, and reshape the fabric of our reality.

The denial of voting and human rights to specific groups stands as a stark reminder of the fragility of democracy and the necessity to safeguard its principles. But in understanding the long-term impact of such denial, we are motivated to uphold the values of inclusivity, representation, and equal opportunity.

"Mastering the Power of Belief" invites us to explore the depths of our convictions, to question, challenge, and embrace the transformative potential within us. It beckons us to find the delicate balance between certainty and doubt, empowering us with intellectual humility and open-mindedness.

Together, we venture into the heart of belief, where the interplay of personal beliefs and collective narratives intertwine. The great Doctor invites us to envision a future where belief unites us, propelling us towards a world that cherishes diversity, justice, and shared progress.

As we immerse ourselves in the richness of these pages, let us be reminded that belief is not a static entity but a dynamic force, responsive to our collective consciousness. May "Mastering the Power of Belief" serve as a guiding light, illuminating the path towards a world where the power of belief is harnessed for the greater good of humanity. (By Dr. David Morgan PhD}

Introduction

"Mastering the Power of Belief"

In the labyrinth of human consciousness lies a force that has shaped civilizations, ignited revolutions, and transformed destinies - belief. From the dawn of time, belief has been an inseparable companion of human experience, guiding our perceptions, influencing our choices, and sculpting the narratives of our existence.

"Mastering the Power of Belief" embarks on a profound exploration of this intangible yet mighty force, weaving together the threads of psychology, sociology, history, and philosophy to unravel the enigma of belief. Within these pages, we embark on a transformative journey, delving into the diverse realms where belief exerts its influence and the profound impact it wields on the trajectory of our lives and the world around us.

In part one, we peer through the annals of history to discern how belief has shaped the tapestry of human lives over the last century. We witness the ripples of belief that have surged through societies, molding cultures, toppling empires, and kindling the fires of progress and enlightenment.

As we venture into part two, we delve deeper into the very essence of belief - its elusive nature and the sources from which it emerges. We unlock the secrets of belief's origin, discovering how it is more than just an abstract idea but a mental state that has the power to influence our attitudes, behaviors, and the very course of our destinies.

Part three opens the gateway to belief's profound impact on spiritual and religious landscapes. We explore the solace and purpose that belief in higher powers provides to individuals and communities, inviting our readers to reflect on the profound connection between belief and the human spirit.

In part four, we embark on an illuminating journey into the realm of scientific rationality, contrasting belief based on faith with convictions grounded in empirical evidence. We confront the interplay between reason and intuition, acknowledging how both can shape our convictions and influence our perceptions of reality.

Throughout our exploration, we unravel the complex ways in which authority figures wield the power to shape belief systems. From academia to politics, we encounter the potency of belief in shaping societies, institutions, and collective narratives.

We confront the paradoxical role of belief as a coping mechanism in times of uncertainty and adversity, seeking comfort and hope while also facing the challenges of confirmation bias and the resistance to question our own beliefs.

As we delve into the societal impact of belief, we examine the role of media and information sources in shaping collective narratives and influencing belief formation. We encounter the perils of misinformation and explore ways to navigate the ever-changing landscape of information dissemination.

The intimate link between belief and personal identity is explored in the pages of this book, shedding light on how our convictions become entwined with how we perceive ourselves and interact with others. We confront the influence of social identity on belief, understanding how our sense of belonging drives our convictions and molds our worldview.

"Mastering the Power of Belief" compels us to question our own beliefs and embrace the significance of critical thinking. We uncover the profound implications of striking a balance between certainty and doubt, cultivating intellectual humility and open-mindedness as essential tools for personal growth and societal progress.

The journey of belief takes us from the visionaries who have sparked revolutions to the technological marvels that have propelled humanity forward. From the struggles for civil rights to the pivotal role of collective beliefs in shaping the rise and fall of nations, we witness the transformative power of belief throughout history.

As we traverse the pages of this book, we confront the challenges posed by the erosion of trust, the suppression of voting and human rights, and the polarization of society. We recognize that safeguarding democratic values and promoting inclusivity are crucial in preserving the integrity of our democratic systems.

The power of belief is a double-edged sword, capable of fostering unity or division, enlightenment or deception. It beckons us to confront our own beliefs, challenge biases, and embrace the diverse tapestry of human experience.

"Mastering the Power of Belief" is an invitation to embark on a journey of self-discovery, collective growth, and societal transformation. It urges us to wield the power of belief with mindfulness and compassion, empowering us to build a world where belief serves as a catalyst for progress, unity, and the pursuit of a brighter tomorrow.

As we begin this profound expedition into the heart of belief, let us embark with an open mind and a willingness to explore the depths of our convictions, for it is through the mastery of belief that we may chart a course towards a world that celebrates our shared humanity and embraces the power of collective imagination.

Author Preface

My dear readers and friends, as I embark on this journey to explore the profound intricacies of belief in "Mastering the Power of Belief," I am humbled by the vastness of the subject and the myriad ways it has shaped human existence throughout history. This book is an endeavor to unravel the threads of conviction that have woven themselves into the fabric of our societies, our minds, and our hearts.

Belief is a force that moves mountains and transforms lives. It is a phenomenon that touches every aspect of our existence, from our personal aspirations to our collective destiny. The power of belief is evident in the pages of history, where it has fueled revolutions, sparked innovations, and fueled the flames of progress.

Yet, belief is a double-edged sword. While it has been a driving force for positive change, it has also been responsible for perpetuating dogmas, division, and injustice. As we navigate through this exploration, we confront the complexities of belief's impact, both as a unifying force and a potential source of adversity.

In this book, we delve into the wellsprings of belief, from religion and spirituality to scientific rationality. We unravel the intricate web of factors that influence belief formation, from authority figures to societal norms, and the power of conditioning that cements our convictions.

We confront the paradox of belief as both a coping mechanism during adversity and a potential source of confirmation bias that obstructs growth. We peer into the influence of media and the role of information dissemination in shaping collective narratives, reflecting on the implications of misinformation and bias.

Through the pages of "Mastering the Power of Belief," we grapple with profound questions. What happens when truth becomes subjective, and lies are normalized? How does the suppression of voting and human rights impact the very essence of democracy? What role does belief play in shaping our understanding of reality, society, and our place in the world?

This book is not a definitive answer to these questions; rather, it is an invitation to embark on a journey of introspection, critical thinking, and self-discovery. It is a call to engage with the complexities of belief, challenge our assumptions, and ultimately cultivate a more profound understanding of ourselves and the world around us.

As we navigate the terrain of belief, let us journey together with an open mind and a willingness to embrace the diversity of human experiences. "Mastering the Power of Belief" is an exploration of the human spirit, a quest to understand the forces that drive us, and a commitment to harness the power of belief for a more just, inclusive, and compassionate world.

I urge each of you to open your minds and hearts as you journey with me through the pages of this book and experience "Mastering the Power of Belief." Let us embark on this voyage of exploration together, ready to challenge our perspectives, question our convictions, and embrace the transformative potential that lies within the realm of belief. As we traverse the diverse landscapes of history, psychology, spirituality, and society, may we emerge with a deeper understanding of the intricate tapestry of human existence and a renewed commitment to shaping a future where belief becomes a force for unity, empathy, and positive change.

PART I
INTRODUCTION
How Belief Has Changed Our Lives Over the

Last 100 Years

Over the past century, humanity has witnessed an extraordinary evolution in various spheres of life, and at the heart of this transformation lies belief. The beliefs we hold collectively and individually have played a pivotal role in shaping the course of history, molding societies, and driving monumental progress. In this chapter, we will explore the profound impact belief has had on the world over the last 100 years, and how it continues to influence our present and future.

The Power of Visionaries: The beliefs of visionary leaders and innovators have fueled groundbreaking advancements, from technological marvels to social revolutions. We will delve into the lives of influential figures who harnessed the power of belief to bring about extraordinary change.

From Horse-Drawn Carriages to Space Exploration: Witness how shifting beliefs about science and human potential have led to unprecedented achievements, propelling us from the simplicity of horse-drawn carriages to the marvels of space exploration and interstellar discoveries.

Challenging Social Norms: Explore the role of belief in challenging social norms and advocating for equality and human rights. Learn about pivotal movements that reshaped societal attitudes and paved the way for inclusivity.

Belief in the Face of Adversity: Uncover stories of individuals and communities who overcame immense challenges through unwavering belief in themselves and their resilience. These tales of triumph will inspire you to face your obstacles with renewed determination.

Technological Paradigm Shifts: Trace the transformative power of belief in the technology sector, where paradigm shifts and groundbreaking innovations have redefined the way we live, work, and communicate.

Belief and Health: Examine the link between belief and health, as medical advancements and the placebo effect demonstrate the influence of belief on healing and well-being.

From Segregation to Integration: Analyze the impact of changing beliefs on race relations and the gradual transition from segregation to integration, paving the way for a more inclusive and united society.

The Power of Collective Belief: Explore how shared beliefs have led to the rise and fall of nations, the formation of alliances, and the pursuit of common goals on a global scale.

Challenging Scientific Dogmas: We delve into the history of scientific discoveries that shattered long-held beliefs and paved the way for revolutionary breakthroughs.

Belief in the Digital Age: We investigate how the digital revolution has shaped belief systems, altered information dissemination, and transformed the way we perceive reality.

The Changing Face of Spirituality: Witness the shift in religious and spiritual beliefs over the last century, reflecting changing attitudes towards faith and a deeper understanding of interconnectedness.

Belief in the Future: Imagine the world of tomorrow, as belief continues to be a driving force behind our aspirations for a better and more sustainable future.

Overcoming Global Challenges: We examine how belief in collective responsibility can drive efforts to tackle pressing global challenges, such as climate change and poverty.

Cultural Impact of Belief: We uncover how beliefs have influenced art, literature, and cultural expressions, shaping the narratives that define our identities.

Lessons from the Past, Visions for the Future: We reflect on the lessons we can learn from the past century, as we envision a future where the power of belief leads us towards greater unity, compassion, and progress.

As we journey through these moments of transformation, we will uncover the threads that connect human belief with the tapestry of history. From the technological marvels that surround us to the societal progress we have achieved, belief stands as the ever-present catalyst that propels us forward. Let us now delve into the chapters that illustrate the profound impact of belief in shaping the world as we know it today.

CHAPTER I

The Power of Visionaries

Visionary leaders and innovators have a unique ability to harness the power of belief and turn their ideas into reality, leading to groundbreaking advancements and transformative changes in various fields. These individuals possess a clear and inspiring vision for the future, driven by strong beliefs and convictions. They are driven by the desire to make a difference and challenge the status quo, and their unwavering belief in their ideas empowers them to overcome obstacles and achieve extraordinary feats.

1. Vision and Inspiration: Visionaries have a clear and compelling vision of what they want to achieve. Their belief in this vision serves as a source of inspiration for themselves and those around them, rallying support and dedication to their cause.

2. Overcoming Challenges: Visionaries often encounter significant challenges and resistance as they introduce new ideas and innovations. Their deep-rooted belief in the potential impact of their vision gives them the resilience and determination to overcome these obstacles.

3. Transformative Innovations: The beliefs of visionar-

ies drive them to explore new possibilities and create transformative innovations. From technological breakthroughs to social revolutions, their commitment to their beliefs fosters groundbreaking advancements.

4. Social and Cultural Change: Many visionary leaders have driven social and cultural change by challenging existing norms and advocating for equality, justice, and human rights. Their beliefs in a better and more just society have ignited social movements and inspired positive change.

5. Influence on Others: The unwavering belief of visionaries can be contagious, influencing and inspiring others to embrace their ideas and join their cause. Their ability to communicate their beliefs effectively fosters a shared sense of purpose among their followers.

6. Reshaping Industries: Visionaries in the business world have transformed industries by challenging conventional practices and introducing disruptive innovations. Their belief in new business models and technologies has reshaped markets and created new opportunities.

7. Empowering Teams: Visionary leaders empower their teams by instilling a sense of purpose and shared beliefs. They create a cohesive and motivated workforce dedicated to achieving a common vision.

8. Legacy of Change: The beliefs of visionaries have a lasting impact that extends beyond their lifetimes. Their achievements become part of their legacy, inspiring future generations and influencing the course of history.

9. The Courage to Take Risks: Visionaries are often willing to take risks and venture into uncharted territory. Their belief in the potential rewards of their actions outweighs the fear of failure, driving them to pursue audacious goals.

10. Empowering Individuals: Visionaries empower individuals to believe in their own potential to make a difference. By witnessing the achievements of visionary leaders, people are encouraged to pursue their own dreams and contribute to positive change.

The power of belief in the lives of visionaries demonstrates the potential of human creativity, determination, and resilience. By exploring the stories of influential figures who have harnessed the power of belief, we gain insights into how convictions can lead to transformative change and inspire a better future for all. These visionaries serve as reminders of the profound impact of beliefs on human progress and the capacity of individuals to shape the world through their unwavering commitment to their ideas

CHAPTER 2

From Horse-Drawn Carriages to Space Exploration

The journey from horse-drawn carriages to space exploration represents a remarkable transformation in human history, driven by shifting beliefs about science, technology, and human potential. Over the centuries, changing perspectives on the nature of the universe and our place in it have paved the way for unprecedented achievements that have revolutionized our lives and expanded our understanding of the cosmos.

1. Renaissance and Scientific Revolution: The Renaissance marked a turning point in human history, emphasizing the importance of reason, observation, and inquiry. This cultural shift laid the foundation for the Scientific Revolution, challenging traditional beliefs and encouraging systematic investigations into the natural world.

2. Enlightenment and Age of Reason: The Enlightenment further fueled a spirit of intellectual inquiry, advocating for rationalism and empirical evidence as the basis for knowledge. This era laid the groundwork for advancements in science, mathematics, and technology.

3. Industrial Revolution and Transportation: The

Industrial Revolution brought about significant technological advancements, including steam engines and the mechanization of transportation. The shift from horse-drawn carriages to steam-powered trains and automobiles revolutionized travel and transportation.

4. Space Exploration and Space Race: In the 20th century, the belief in the potential of space exploration became a reality. The Space Race between the United States and the Soviet Union drove unprecedented achievements, leading to the first human landing on the Moon in 1969.

5. Technological Innovations: Advances in science and technology, driven by belief in human potential, have enabled space missions to explore distant planets, send robotic probes beyond our solar system, and even capture images of black holes.

6. Expanding Frontiers: Shifting beliefs about human potential have led to the exploration of the outer reaches of our solar system and beyond. Space missions like Voyager and New Horizons continue to expand our understanding of the universe.

7. The Hubble Space Telescope: The Hubble Space Telescope, launched in 1990, has provided unprecedented views of distant galaxies, nebulae, and other celestial phenomena, reshaping our understanding

of the cosmos.

8. International Collaboration: Space exploration has become a platform for international collaboration, demonstrating how shared beliefs in scientific progress and human potential can bring nations together for peaceful purposes.

9. Interstellar Discoveries: Advances in astronomy and technology have led to the discovery of exoplanets and potential habitable zones in distant star systems, igniting the search for extraterrestrial life.

10. Future Frontiers: As technology and scientific understanding continue to evolve, the belief in human potential pushes us to consider even grander frontiers, such as interstellar travel and the colonization of other planets.

The journey from horse-drawn carriages to space exploration exemplifies the power of shifting beliefs in shaping human progress. Believing in the potential of science, reason, and human ingenuity has led to revolutionary advancements that were once unimaginable. The marvels of space exploration and the quest for interstellar discoveries reflect our insatiable curiosity and the boundless belief in our ability to explore the universe and our place within it. These achievements stand as a testament to the extraordinary height's humanity can reach when we embrace the power of belief and pursue the unknown with passion and determination.

CHAPTER 3

Challenging Social Norms

Belief plays a critical role in challenging social norms and advocating for equality and human rights. Throughout history, pivotal movements driven by strong convictions have reshaped societal attitudes, breaking down barriers, and fostering inclusivity. These movements are fueled by the belief in justice, fairness, and the potential to create positive change for marginalized communities and oppressed individuals.

1. Civil Rights Movement: The Civil Rights Movement in the United States during the 1950s and 1960s challenged racial segregation and discrimination against African Americans. Leaders like Dr. Martin Luther King Jr., Rosa Parks, and Malcolm X inspired millions with their belief in racial equality and justice. Their efforts led to significant legal and social changes, advancing civil rights and fostering a more inclusive society.

2. Suffrage Movement: The suffrage movement advocated for women's right to vote. The belief in gender equality and women's empowerment spurred suffragettes to challenge social norms, leading to the eventual granting of voting rights to women in many countries.

3. LGBTQ+ Rights Movement: The LGBTQ+ rights movement has challenged societal norms surrounding gender and sexual orientation. Activists, through their unwavering belief in LGBTQ+ rights, have fought for legal recognition, anti-discrimination protections, and social acceptance.

4. Disability Rights Movement: The disability rights movement advocates for equal opportunities and accessibility for people with disabilities. It challenges societal norms that often marginalize and exclude individuals with disabilities, aiming for inclusivity and equal treatment.

5. Human Rights Campaigns: Human rights campaigns across the globe address various issues, such as child labor, access to education, healthcare, and freedom from discrimination. These movements are driven by the belief in the inherent dignity and worth of every individual.

6. Environmental Activism: Environmental activists challenge social norms related to consumption, waste, and unsustainable practices. Their belief in environmental stewardship and the urgency to address climate change has sparked global movements for a sustainable future.

7. Indigenous Rights Movements: Indigenous rights movements advocate for the recognition and protection of indigenous peoples' rights, cultural heritage, and land. They challenge historical injustices and seek to preserve indigenous knowledge and way of life.

8. Intersectionality: Many social justice movements recognize the importance of intersectionality—the interconnectedness of various forms of oppression and discrimination. The belief in intersectionality underscores the need for inclusive and holistic approaches to social change.

9. Public Awareness and Education: Believers in social justice often work to raise public awareness and educate others about issues related to equality and human rights. This empowers individuals to challenge ingrained prejudices and become advocates for positive change.

10. Policy Advocacy: Belief in social change often leads to policy advocacy, where activists work to influence laws and institutional practices to create a more just and equitable society.

Challenging social norms and advocating for equality and human rights requires immense courage, resilience, and unwavering belief in the possibility of a better future. These movements have reshaped societal attitudes, laws, and policies, driving progress towards more inclusive, diverse, and compassionate communities. The power of belief in the inherent worth and rights of every individual has been instrumental in breaking down barriers and fostering a world where everyone can live with dignity and equal opportunities.

CHAPTER 4
Belief in the Face of Adversity

Throughout history, there are countless inspiring stories of individuals and communities who have faced immense challenges with unwavering belief in themselves and their resilience. These tales of triumph demonstrate the power of belief in overcoming obstacles, instilling hope, and transforming lives.

1. Anne Frank: Anne Frank, a Jewish girl during the Holocaust, kept a diary while in hiding from the Nazis. Despite facing the darkest of circumstances, her belief in the power of her words and the resilience of the human spirit shines through in her writings. Her diary has become a testament to hope and the indomitable belief in the face of adversity.

2. Nelson Mandela: Nelson Mandela, a leader in the fight against apartheid in South Africa, spent 27 years in prison. Despite the harsh conditions and long confinement, his unwavering belief in justice, equality, and forgiveness helped him emerge from prison to become the country's first black president.

3. Malala Yousafzai: Malala Yousafzai, a young advocate for girls' education in Pakistan, survived a brutal attack

by the Taliban. Her belief in the power of education and her unwavering commitment to fighting for girls' rights propelled her to become the youngest-ever Nobel Prize laureate.

4. Helen Keller: Despite being deaf and blind from a young age, Helen Keller's belief in her potential and the capacity of others to understand her abilities drove her to become a renowned author, political activist, and lecturer. Her story demonstrates the strength of belief in oneself and the human spirit.

5. The Civil Rights Movement: The Civil Rights Movement in the United States faced tremendous adversity as activists fought for racial equality and an end to segregation and discrimination. Their collective belief in the power of nonviolent resistance and their unyielding commitment to justice brought about significant social change.

6. The Rwandan Genocide Survivors: The survivors of the Rwandan genocide faced unimaginable horrors and loss. Despite their deep scars, many of them exhibited tremendous resilience and belief in rebuilding their lives and communities, fostering reconciliation, and healing.

7. The Apollo 13 Mission: The Apollo 13 mission faced

a life-threatening crisis in space, but the belief in the expertise and determination of the astronauts and the ground team led to a miraculous return to Earth, highlighting the power of human ingenuity and teamwork.

8. Refugee Stories: Countless refugees around the world have overcome extraordinary hardships, fleeing violence and persecution. Their belief in the possibility of a better life and their resilience in adapting to new environments inspire hope and perseverance.

9. Communities in Disaster Recovery: Communities affected by natural disasters, such as hurricanes, earthquakes, or tsunamis, have demonstrated incredible strength and belief in rebuilding their lives and rebuilding their communities in the aftermath of destruction.

10. Paralympic Athletes: Paralympic athletes face physical challenges but demonstrate incredible belief in their abilities and the power of determination. Their achievements in sports showcase the strength of belief and the triumph of the human spirit over adversity.

These stories of triumph in the face of adversity show us the remarkable capacity of belief to fuel determination, resilience, and hope. They remind us that no matter how daunting the obstacles may seem, believing in ourselves and our potential can lead to transformative outcomes. Through unwavering belief, individuals and communities have turned tragedy into triumph, showing us that with the right mindset, we can overcome even the most challenging circumstances.

CHAPTER 5
Technological Paradigm Shifts

The technology sector has been marked by transformative paradigm shifts, driven by the belief in the potential of innovation and the power of human ingenuity. These shifts have brought about groundbreaking advancements that have reshaped every aspect of human life, from communication and industry to healthcare and education. The evolution of technology showcases how belief in progress and the capacity to solve problems has led to a world that is vastly different from what it once was.

1. The Digital Revolution: The belief in the potential of computers and digital technology sparked the Digital Revolution. The development of microprocessors and the creation of the first personal computers paved the way for a new era of information processing and connectivity.

2. The Internet Age: The belief in a globally connected world led to the development of the internet. The birth of the World Wide Web revolutionized communication, commerce, and access to information, bringing people from different parts of the world closer together.

3. Mobile Technology: The belief in mobility and convenience drove the development of mobile technology. The introduction of smartphones and tablets transformed how people interact with information, applications, and each other, making communication and computing accessible anytime, anywhere.

4. Artificial Intelligence (AI): The belief in the potential of machines to simulate human intelligence led to the development of AI. From virtual assistants to sophisticated machine learning algorithms, AI is transforming industries and revolutionizing the way we approach problem-solving.

5. Internet of Things (IoT): The belief in the interconnectedness of devices and objects gave rise to the Internet of Things. IoT enables smart homes, smart cities, and seamless integration of technology into various aspects of daily life.

6. Renewable Energy: The belief in sustainable and eco-friendly solutions spurred the development of renewable energy technologies. Innovations in solar, wind, and other renewable energy sources are transforming the energy landscape and addressing environmental challenges.

7. Biotechnology and Medical Advances: The belief in the potential of science to improve human health has led to significant advancements in biotechnology and medicine. From gene editing to personalized medicine, these innovations are changing the way we approach healthcare.

8. E-Commerce and Digital Transformation: The belief in the potential of online commerce has revolutionized retail and business practices. E-commerce platforms and digital transformation have reshaped how companies operate and how consumers shop.

9. Virtual and Augmented Reality: The belief in creating immersive experiences drove the development of virtual and augmented reality technologies. These innovations have applications in gaming, training, education, and beyond.

10. Space Exploration and Colonization: The belief in exploring the cosmos and establishing a presence beyond Earth has driven advancements in space exploration. Private space companies and international collaborations are pushing the boundaries of human space travel and colonization.

The technological paradigm shifts we have witnessed demonstrate the transformative power of belief in human progress. By embracing innovation and having faith in our ability to overcome challenges, we have witnessed advancements that were once only the stuff of science fiction. The evolution of technology continues to shape our world, and the belief in the potential of human ingenuity remains at the heart of these remarkable changes. As we move forward, the power of belief will continue to drive us to explore new frontiers and tackle the most pressing challenges of our time.

CHAPTER 6
Belief and Health

The link between belief and health is a fascinating and complex area of study that highlights the profound influence of our mental and emotional states on our physical well-being. Both medical advancements and the placebo effect provide valuable insights into the ways in which belief can impact healing and overall health.

1. Placebo Effect: The placebo effect is a well-known phenomenon where individuals experience improvements in their health simply because they believe they are receiving a beneficial treatment. Placebos, which are inert substances with no therapeutic value, can lead to real and measurable health improvements when patients believe they are receiving an effective medication.

2. Mind-Body Connection: The placebo effect underscores the mind-body connection, demonstrating that the beliefs and expectations of patients can influence their physiological responses and healing processes. Positive beliefs and optimism can trigger the release of endorphins and other neurotransmitters, promoting feelings of well-being and potentially enhancing recovery.

3. Psychological Factors: Beliefs, attitudes, and emotional states play a significant role in managing chronic conditions, coping with illness, and overall health outcomes. Optimism, hope, and a sense of control over one's health have been linked to better treatment adherence and overall quality of life.

4. Placebo Surgery: In some cases, even sham surgeries (placebo surgeries) have been shown to yield improvements in patients' conditions. This further highlights the power of belief and the psychological aspects of healing.

5. Nocebo Effect: Conversely, negative beliefs and expectations can lead to the "nocebo effect," where patients experience adverse effects or worsened symptoms due to negative beliefs about a treatment or medication.

6. Integrative Medicine: The field of integrative medicine recognizes the importance of addressing the psychological and emotional aspects of health alongside traditional medical interventions. Incorporating practices like mindfulness, meditation, and positive visualization can complement medical treatments and support healing.

7. Patient-Provider Communication: The way healthcare

providers communicate with patients can influence their beliefs and expectations about treatments. Empathetic and supportive communication can positively impact patient outcomes.

8. Medical Advancements: Medical advancements have historically been driven by a belief in the potential to improve health and save lives. Breakthroughs in medicine and technology have led to better treatments, disease prevention, and increased life expectancy.

9. Mindfulness and Stress Reduction: Mindfulness practices have been linked to reduced stress, improved immune function, and better overall health. Cultivating a sense of calm and well-being through mindfulness can positively impact various health conditions.

10. Belief in Self-Healing: The belief in the body's ability to heal itself, coupled with appropriate medical care, can foster a positive mindset and contribute to the healing process.

The connection between belief and health highlights the importance of a holistic approach to well-being, where physical health, emotional well-being, and mental attitudes are all considered integral components of health care. Recognizing the power of belief can lead to more patient-centered and integrative approaches to healthcare, emphasizing the importance of positive beliefs, support, and empathy in fostering healing and improving overall health outcomes.

CHAPTER 7
From Segregation to Integration

The transition from segregation to integration in race relations has been a pivotal journey driven by changing beliefs and societal attitudes. Historically, racial segregation enforced strict separation and discrimination based on race, leading to profound injustices and inequalities. However, evolving beliefs and the tireless efforts of civil rights activists have paved the way for a more inclusive and united society, where integration and equality are championed.

1. Historical Context: Racial segregation was deeply ingrained in many societies, with laws and policies enforcing separate facilities, schools, and public spaces for different racial groups. The belief in racial superiority and inferiority perpetuated discriminatory practices.

2. Civil Rights Movement: The Civil Rights Movement, particularly in the United States, challenged racial segregation and advocated for equal rights and opportunities for African Americans. Influential leaders like Dr. Martin Luther King Jr. and Rosa Parks spearheaded nonviolent protests and inspired a nationwide call for racial justice.

3. Changing Public Opinion: Over time, changing beliefs and public opinion shifted towards recognizing the inherent dignity and equality of all individuals, regardless of race. Awareness of the injustices of segregation grew, leading to increased support for integration.

4. Legal Transformations: Landmark court decisions, such as Brown v. Board of Education in the United States, declared racial segregation unconstitutional, catalyzing significant legal changes and opening the path to integration.

5. Desegregation of Institutions: Educational institutions, public facilities, and workplaces gradually desegregated, promoting integration and equality in previously segregated spaces.

6. Role of Media and Communication: The media played a crucial role in shaping beliefs about racial integration. Coverage of civil rights struggles and stories of racial injustice increased public awareness and fostered empathy.

7. Advocacy and Grassroots Movements: Grassroots movements, community organizing, and advocacy efforts furthered the cause of racial integration, promoting dialogue and fostering alliances across

racial lines.

8. Cultural Shifts: Changing cultural norms and beliefs contributed to racial integration, as artists, writers, and musicians highlighted the importance of racial harmony and equality through their works.

9. Diversity and Inclusion Policies: Integration efforts extended to the workplace and public institutions, with diversity and inclusion policies aiming to create more equitable environments.

10. Continuing Challenges: Despite significant progress, challenges to racial integration persist, requiring ongoing commitment to address systemic racism and promote equality.

The transition from segregation to integration highlights the transformative power of changing beliefs and the collective efforts of individuals and communities. It demonstrates that progress towards a more inclusive society is possible when the values of equality, empathy, and social justice take precedence over discriminatory beliefs. While the journey towards full integration and racial harmony continues, recognizing the historical strides made towards a more united society reminds us of the importance of continuously challenging prejudices and working towards a future where diversity is embraced and celebrated. The impact of changing beliefs on race relations serves as a testament to the potential for positive social change when individuals and communities unite in the pursuit of equality and justice for all.

CHAPTER 8
The Power of Collective Belief

Collective belief, the shared set of values, principles, and ideologies held by a group of people, has been a driving force throughout history, shaping the destiny of nations, alliances, and global movements. It has the power to unify people, create a sense of identity and purpose, and propel them towards common goals. The impact of collective belief is evident in the rise and fall of civilizations, the formation of alliances, and the pursuit of common objectives on a global scale.

1. Nation-Building and Identity: Collective belief plays a pivotal role in nation-building, forging a shared identity among diverse populations. It unites people under a common flag, language, and cultural heritage, fostering a sense of unity and loyalty to the nation.

2. Revolutions and Independence Movements: Collective belief in freedom, justice, and autonomy has sparked revolutions and independence movements, leading to the overthrow of oppressive regimes and the birth of new nations.

3. Ideological Movements: Throughout history, ideological movements based on collective belief, such

as communism, fascism, and democracy, have shaped political systems and governance structures around the world.

4. Alliances and Coalitions: Shared beliefs often lead to the formation of alliances and coalitions between nations. These partnerships are based on common interests, values, and goals, enhancing diplomatic, economic, and military cooperation.

5. Religious Movements: Religious beliefs have been instrumental in shaping civilizations and fostering collective identities among adherents. They have motivated great social and cultural shifts and inspired humanitarian efforts.

6. Global Movements: Global movements, such as human rights advocacy, environmental conservation, and gender equality, are driven by collective beliefs in justice, sustainability, and equality.

7. Economic Growth and Development: Collective belief in economic progress and development has driven nations and communities to invest in infrastructure, education, and innovation, spurring economic growth.

8. Conflict and Wars: Conflicts and wars often arise from conflicting collective beliefs, such as competing territorial claims or ideological differences. The clash of

beliefs can lead to long-lasting geopolitical tensions.

9. Cultural Influence and Soft Power: Nations with strong cultural beliefs and values often wield significant soft power, influencing others through their art, literature, and cultural exports.

10. Response to Global Challenges: Collective belief can mobilize nations to address global challenges like climate change, pandemics, and poverty through international cooperation and joint initiatives.

The power of collective belief lies in its ability to mobilize and unite people towards a common purpose. It can drive individuals to make sacrifices for the greater good and create a sense of community and belonging. However, collective belief can also be a double-edged sword, leading to conflict and division when different groups hold opposing beliefs.

The impact of collective belief on a global scale underscores the significance of promoting understanding, dialogue, and cooperation between nations and cultures. By recognizing the diverse beliefs that shape our world, we can strive for a more inclusive and harmonious global community, where shared values, empathy, and cooperation foster a sustainable and prosperous future for all.

CHAPTER 9
Challenging Scientific Dogmas

Throughout history, there have been numerous instances where scientific discoveries challenged long-held beliefs and overturned established dogmas. These breakthroughs revolutionized our understanding of the natural world, opening new frontiers of knowledge and reshaping scientific paradigms. Here are some examples of groundbreaking discoveries that shattered scientific dogmas:

1. Heliocentrism: In the 16th century, Nicolaus Copernicus proposed the heliocentric model of the solar system, which challenged the prevailing belief that the Earth was the center of the universe. His work laid the foundation for the modern understanding of planetary motion and celestial mechanics.

2. Evolution by Natural Selection: Charles Darwin's theory of evolution by natural selection, presented in his seminal work "On the Origin of Species" in 1859, challenged the prevailing religious beliefs about the creation of species. Darwin's theory provided a scientific explanation for the diversity of life on Earth.

3. Germ Theory of Disease: In the 19th century, Louis

Pasteur and Robert Koch challenged the miasma theory of disease, which held that diseases were caused by "bad air." They proposed the germ theory of disease, demonstrating that microorganisms were responsible for many infectious illnesses.

4. Quantum Mechanics: In the early 20th century, the discovery of quantum mechanics challenged classical physics and our understanding of the behavior of matter and energy at the atomic and subatomic level. Pioneers like Max Planck, Albert Einstein, and Niels Bohr revolutionized our view of the universe.

5. Relativity Theory: Albert Einstein's theory of relativity, published in 1905 (special relativity) and 1915 (general relativity), challenged the Newtonian view of absolute space and time. Einstein's theories showed that the fabric of spacetime could be affected by gravity and motion.

6. Plate Tectonics: In the mid-20th century, the theory of plate tectonics challenged the long-standing belief in static continents. This theory proposed that the Earth's lithosphere is divided into tectonic plates that move and interact, causing earthquakes, volcanic activity, and the formation of mountain ranges.

7. Big Bang Theory: The Big Bang theory, proposed in

the 20th century, challenged the belief in a steady-state universe. This theory suggests that the universe began from a hot, dense state and has been expanding ever since.

8. Human Genome Project: The completion of the Human Genome Project in 2003 challenged the deterministic view of genetics. It revealed that human genes interact with the environment, leading to a more nuanced understanding of genetics and human traits.

9. Exoplanets and Search for Extraterrestrial Life: The discovery of exoplanets outside our solar system challenged the belief that our solar system was unique. This discovery has fueled the search for extraterrestrial life and expanded our perspective on the possibility of life beyond Earth.

10. Gravitational Waves: The detection of gravitational waves in 2015, predicted by Einstein's general theory of relativity, provided direct evidence of ripples in spacetime, confirming one of the last unverified predictions of the theory.

These examples demonstrate the dynamic nature of science and the importance of challenging prevailing beliefs to advance our understanding of the natural world. Scientific progress often hinges on the willingness of researchers to question established dogmas and embrace new ideas and evidence. The history of these revolutionary discoveries serves as a testament to the power of human curiosity, creativity, and the pursuit of knowledge in expanding the frontiers of science.

CHAPTER 10
Belief in the Digital Age

The digital revolution, marked by the widespread adoption of digital technologies and the internet, has profoundly shaped belief systems, altered information dissemination, and transformed the way we perceive reality. The rapid evolution of technology has had both positive and negative effects on the formation and dissemination of beliefs in the digital age.

1. Information Access: The internet has democratized access to information, allowing people from diverse backgrounds to explore a wide range of perspectives. However, the abundance of information can also lead to information overload and the challenge of discerning credible sources.

2. Echo Chambers and Filter Bubbles: Digital platforms and algorithms can create echo chambers and filter bubbles, where individuals are exposed only to information that aligns with their existing beliefs. This can reinforce preexisting beliefs and limit exposure to diverse viewpoints.

3. Disinformation and Misinformation: The ease of sharing information online has also given rise to the

spread of disinformation and misinformation. False or misleading content can spread rapidly, leading to the formation of beliefs based on inaccurate information.

4. Social Media Influence: Social media platforms play a significant role in shaping beliefs and opinions. Viral content and influencers can sway public sentiment and influence belief systems.

5. Confirmation Bias: Digital platforms can amplify confirmation bias, where individuals seek out and believe information that confirms their preexisting beliefs while dismissing contradictory evidence.

6. Globalization of Beliefs: The digital age has facilitated the global exchange of ideas and beliefs, leading to the convergence and cross-pollination of cultural, religious, and ideological beliefs.

7. Online Communities and Belonging: The internet has enabled the formation of online communities based on shared beliefs, interests, and identities. These communities can foster a sense of belonging and solidarity among like-minded individuals.

8. Citizen Journalism and Grassroots Movements: Digital technology has empowered citizen journalism and grassroots movements, providing a platform for individuals to voice their beliefs, advocate for causes,

and mobilize for social change.

9. Online Radicalization: The digital age has also witnessed instances of online radicalization, where individuals are exposed to extremist beliefs and ideologies through online channels.

10. Virtual Reality and Augmented Reality: Advancements in virtual and augmented reality technologies have the potential to further blur the lines between digital and physical reality, shaping belief systems and perceptions in new and immersive ways.

The digital age has redefined the landscape of belief formation, dissemination, and perception. While it has democratized information access and provided opportunities for connection and advocacy, it has also posed challenges related to misinformation, echo chambers, and digital manipulation. As the digital revolution continues to evolve, understanding and critically evaluating the impact of digital technologies on belief systems will be crucial in fostering a well-informed, inclusive, and balanced digital society. Promoting media literacy, critical thinking, and ethical information sharing are essential steps towards navigating the complexities of belief in the digital age.

CHAPTER 11
The Changing Face of Spirituality

Over the last century, there has been a significant shift in religious and spiritual beliefs, reflecting changing attitudes towards faith and a deeper understanding of interconnectedness. Various factors, including advancements in science and technology, globalization, and shifts in societal values, have influenced this transformation in spirituality.

1. Decline in Traditional Religiosity: In many parts of the world, there has been a decline in traditional religious adherence and attendance. People are increasingly identifying as religiously unaffiliated or "spiritual but not religious."

2. Rise of Spiritual Pluralism: As societies become more diverse and interconnected, there has been a rise in spiritual pluralism, where individuals draw inspiration from multiple spiritual traditions, practices, and philosophies.

3. Seekers and Nones: Many individuals are on personal spiritual journeys, exploring different belief systems and seeking to find meaning and purpose in their lives. This has led to the emergence of the "spiritual

but not religious" category and a rise in the number of religiously unaffiliated individuals, often referred to as "nones."

4. Mindfulness and Meditation: Practices like mindfulness and meditation have gained popularity as tools for self-discovery, stress reduction, and spiritual growth. These practices are often incorporated into secular contexts and have been embraced by people of various belief systems.

5. Eco-Spirituality: Concern for the environment and a deeper appreciation of interconnectedness with nature have given rise to eco-spirituality. Many individuals now view nature as sacred and see spirituality as intrinsically linked to environmental stewardship.

6. Interfaith Dialogue: Globalization and increased intercultural interactions have facilitated interfaith dialogue, promoting understanding and appreciation of different religious traditions.

7. New Age Spirituality: New Age spirituality encompasses a wide range of beliefs and practices that often draw on elements from various spiritual traditions, alternative healing methods, and esoteric philosophies.

8. Emphasis on Personal Experience: Many modern spiritual seekers prioritize personal experience and

direct connection to the divine or transcendent, rather than relying solely on authoritative religious institutions.

9. Inclusivity and Acceptance: Changing societal attitudes have led to more inclusive and accepting spiritual communities that embrace diversity in terms of gender, sexual orientation, race, and background.

10. Integration with Science: Some individuals seek to reconcile their spiritual beliefs with scientific understanding, leading to the emergence of fields like "spiritual neuroscience" and "integral spirituality."

This shifting landscape of spirituality reflects a broader trend towards seeking personal meaning, authenticity, and interconnectedness in a rapidly changing world. People are exploring spirituality in ways that resonate with their individual experiences and beliefs, leading to a diverse and multifaceted spiritual landscape. As science continues to advance and society evolves, spirituality will likely continue to adapt and change, reflecting humanity's ongoing quest for understanding, purpose, and connection to something greater than us.

CHAPTER 12
Belief in the Future

In the world of tomorrow, belief will continue to be a driving force behind our aspirations for a better and more sustainable future. As we confront global challenges and embrace technological advancements, the power of belief will shape our collective efforts to create a more inclusive, prosperous, and harmonious world.

1. Technological Advancements: The belief in the potential of technology to address complex problems will drive continuous innovation. Advancements in artificial intelligence, renewable energy, biotechnology, and space exploration will reshape industries and improve the quality of life for people around the globe.

2. Sustainability and Environmental Stewardship: The growing belief in the urgency of environmental preservation will lead to concerted efforts to combat climate change, protect biodiversity, and foster sustainable practices in all aspects of life.

3. Global Collaboration: The belief in the interconnectedness of humanity will promote global collaboration to address transnational challenges such as pandemics, poverty, and migration. International

alliances will form to foster peace, prosperity, and cooperation.

4. Inclusive Societies: The belief in the inherent value of every individual will drive efforts to build inclusive societies that embrace diversity and ensure equal opportunities for all, regardless of background or identity.

5. Empowering Education: The belief in the transformative power of education will lead to enhanced access to quality education worldwide. Technology will facilitate personalized learning, fostering critical thinking and creativity.

6. Health and Well-being: The belief in the importance of physical and mental well-being will inspire comprehensive healthcare systems that prioritize prevention, early intervention, and holistic approaches to health.

7. Space Exploration and Colonization: The belief in humanity's potential to explore and settle beyond Earth will lead to ambitious space exploration missions and the establishment of human colonies on other celestial bodies.

8. Ethical Advancements: The belief in the ethical application of technology and scientific advancements

will shape the development of laws and regulations to ensure responsible innovation and protect individual rights.

9. Empowerment of Communities: The belief in the power of grassroots movements will empower communities to address local challenges, promote social justice, and create positive change from the bottom up.

10. Spirit of Resilience: The belief in the resilience of the human spirit will inspire people to face adversity with determination and optimism, fostering a sense of hope in the face of challenges.

As belief continues to be a guiding force in shaping the future, it will not be without its challenges. We will need to address issues such as misinformation, ideological conflicts, and the ethical implications of new technologies. However, the collective power of belief will drive humanity's progress forward, instilling hope and fostering a shared vision of a better world. By embracing a belief in our capacity to solve global problems and create positive change, we can work together to build a future that is sustainable, inclusive, and built on the principles of compassion, understanding, and empathy. The world of tomorrow, shaped by our collective belief, holds the potential for unprecedented achievements and the realization of dreams that will benefit all of humanity.

CHAPTER 13
Overcoming Global Challenges

Belief in collective responsibility can be a powerful catalyst for driving efforts to tackle pressing global challenges, such as climate change and poverty. When individuals and societies collectively believe in their capacity to effect positive change and recognize their interconnectedness with the world, they are more likely to take meaningful actions to address these challenges. Here's how belief in collective responsibility can lead to impactful solutions:

1. Recognizing Interconnectedness: Belief in collective responsibility fosters an understanding that global challenges are not isolated issues affecting specific regions or communities. Instead, they are interconnected and have far-reaching implications for the entire planet and all its inhabitants.

2. Empathy and Solidarity: Belief in collective responsibility encourages empathy and solidarity with those affected by global challenges. It creates a sense of shared humanity and a commitment to alleviating suffering and inequality worldwide.

3. Global Cooperation and Alliances: When there is a belief

in collective responsibility, nations and communities are more likely to form global alliances and partnerships to pool resources, knowledge, and expertise to address challenges that require international cooperation.

4. Policy Advocacy: Collective belief drives advocacy for policies and regulations that prioritize sustainable practices, poverty alleviation, and environmental conservation on national and international levels.

5. Grassroots Movements: Belief in collective responsibility often leads to the formation of grassroots movements, where individuals and local communities take initiatives to address global challenges at a grassroots level, creating positive change from the ground up.

6. Sustainable Practices and Innovation: Belief in collective responsibility promotes the adoption of sustainable practices in industries, businesses, and daily life. It also encourages investment in research and innovation to develop sustainable technologies and solutions.

7. Education and Awareness: Belief in collective responsibility drives educational initiatives and awareness campaigns to inform people about global challenges and inspire action.

8. Philanthropy and Aid: Individuals and organizations with a belief in collective responsibility are more likely to contribute to philanthropic efforts and provide aid to vulnerable communities affected by poverty, climate disasters, and other challenges.

9. Environmental and Social Justice: Belief in collective responsibility empowers individuals and communities to advocate for environmental and social justice, ensuring that the burden of global challenges does not disproportionately fall on marginalized populations.

10. Long-term Planning: With a belief in collective responsibility, societies are more likely to engage in long-term planning and invest in solutions that will have lasting impacts on addressing global challenges.

By fostering a belief in collective responsibility, we can overcome the barriers of indifference and apathy that hinder progress in addressing pressing global challenges. This shared belief provides a moral imperative to act and empowers people to contribute their skills, resources, and creativity to finding solutions. Embracing the interconnectedness of our world and recognizing our collective responsibility can lead to a future where sustainable practices, poverty eradication, and environmental stewardship are not merely aspirations but achievable goals. As individuals and societies unite around this belief, we can pave the way for a more equitable, resilient, and sustainable world for current and future generations.

CHAPTER 14
Cultural Impact of Belief

Beliefs have a profound and far-reaching impact on culture, influencing art, literature, and various forms of cultural expression. The narratives that arise from these beliefs play a central role in shaping collective identities and reflecting the values and aspirations of societies. Here's how beliefs have influenced cultural expressions and the way they define our identities:

1. Religious Art and Architecture: Religious beliefs have been a significant source of inspiration for art and architecture throughout history. Cathedrals, temples, mosques, and other religious structures stand as masterpieces of human creativity, reflecting the spiritual beliefs and values of different cultures.

2. Mythology and Folklore: Beliefs in deities, heroes, and mythical creatures have given rise to rich mythologies and folklore. These narratives provide insights into the cultural worldview, moral teachings, and historical origins of societies.

3. Literature and Symbolism: Beliefs, whether religious, philosophical, or ideological, have influenced literature across different genres. Themes of redemption,

enlightenment, and destiny often emerge from prevailing beliefs, adding depth and symbolism to literary works.

4. Artistic Representations of the Divine: Beliefs about the divine and the afterlife have inspired countless artistic representations of gods, goddesses, angels, and other spiritual beings. These depictions serve to convey religious teachings and evoke a sense of awe and reverence.

5. Cultural Festivals and Rituals: Cultural beliefs manifest in the form of festivals, rituals, and celebrations that are integral to the identity and heritage of communities. These events reinforce cultural values, foster social cohesion, and create a sense of belonging.

6. Philosophical Inquiry: Beliefs about the nature of existence, morality, and human purpose have influenced philosophical discourse, providing frameworks for understanding the world and human behavior.

7. Political Ideologies: Political beliefs and ideologies have shaped the art and cultural expressions of societies. Revolutionary art, propaganda, and nationalist themes often emerge from political convictions.

8. Social Movements and Activism: Beliefs play a significant role in shaping social movements and

activism. Artists, writers, and cultural icons often use their creative expressions to advocate for social justice, equality, and human rights.

9. Identity Formation: Cultural expressions rooted in beliefs contribute to the formation of individual and collective identities. They help people understand their place in the world, their heritage, and the values they hold dear.

10. Oral Traditions and Storytelling: Beliefs are passed down through generations via oral traditions and storytelling. These narratives serve as a repository of cultural knowledge, reflecting the shared experiences and wisdom of communities.

The cultural impact of belief is a dynamic and evolving process, reflecting the changing beliefs and values of societies over time. It is a continuous dialogue between past and present, tradition and innovation. Cultural expressions influenced by beliefs can reinforce societal norms and reinforce the status quo, but they can also challenge existing paradigms and inspire new ways of thinking.

Understanding the cultural impact of belief allows us to appreciate the richness and diversity of human experience. It invites us to critically examine the narratives that shape our identities and cultural expressions, fostering a deeper understanding of ourselves and others. By recognizing the power of beliefs in shaping culture, we can engage in constructive dialogue, celebrate cultural diversity, and contribute to a more inclusive and interconnected world.

CHAPTER 15

Lessons from the Past, Visions for the Future

Looking back on the past century, there are valuable lessons to be learned that can guide us towards a future where the power of belief leads us to greater unity, compassion, and progress. As we envision this future, here are some key reflections and principles to consider:

1. Lessons in Resilience: The past century has been marked by numerous challenges, including wars, pandemics, economic crises, and social upheavals. However, humanity has shown remarkable resilience in overcoming these difficulties. The belief in our collective strength and determination to persevere can empower us to navigate future challenges with courage and optimism.

2. Embracing Diversity: History has taught us that the world is a tapestry of cultures, beliefs, and perspectives. Embracing diversity and recognizing the value of different viewpoints can foster understanding, empathy, and global cooperation.

3. The Power of Unity: Unity has proven to be a potent force for positive change. When people unite around common beliefs and shared goals, they can overcome seemingly insurmountable obstacles and work together to create a better world.

4. Compassion and Empathy: Empathy and compassion are essential qualities that have the power to bridge divides and heal wounds. By understanding and caring for one another, we can build stronger and more inclusive communities.

5. Progress through Collaboration: History is filled with examples of groundbreaking advancements achieved through collaborative efforts. When individuals and nations come together to share knowledge, resources, and expertise, progress is accelerated and solutions are found.

6. Learning from Mistakes: The past century has seen both triumphs and mistakes. Reflecting on past errors allows us to learn valuable lessons, make better choices, and avoid repeating the same pitfalls in the future.

7. Balancing Tradition and Innovation: The power of belief lies in its ability to adapt to changing times. As we envision the future, we can draw wisdom from tradition while embracing innovation and progress.

8. Environmental Stewardship: The environmental challenges we face today call for a greater sense of responsibility towards the planet. Understanding the impact of our beliefs and actions on the environment can inspire sustainable practices and conservation efforts.

9. Investing in Education: Education has been instrumental in driving progress and societal development. Investing in quality education for all fosters critical thinking, empathy, and the capacity to build a brighter future.

10. A Vision of Hope: Envisioning a future driven by the power of belief should be a vision of hope. By believing in our ability to create positive change, we cultivate a mindset of possibility, inspiring action and shaping a better world for generations to come.

In envisioning a future shaped by the power of belief, it is essential to recognize the interconnectedness of humanity and our shared responsibility to care for one another and the planet we inhabit. A future grounded in unity, compassion, and progress is not a distant dream but a tangible reality that can be built through individual and collective efforts.

By learning from the lessons of the past, we can overcome challenges, celebrate our diversity, and work together to create a future where the power of belief propels us towards greater unity, compassion, and progress. The vision of such a future is not merely aspirational but a call to action, inviting each one of us to be active participants in shaping a world where our beliefs become a force for positive transformation and lasting change.

PART II
INTRODUCTION
Understanding Belief and Its Sources

Belief is a fundamental aspect of human cognition and consciousness. It influences our thoughts, emotions, and actions, shaping the lens through which we perceive the world. In part two, we will delve into the essence of belief, exploring its definition, significance, and the underlying sources that give rise to our convictions.

We begin by unraveling the concept of belief itself. Explore how belief is more than just an abstract idea; it is a mental state that holds the power to influence our attitudes, behaviors, and decisions.

The Role of Perception: Discover the interplay between perception and belief, as our interpretations of reality serve as the foundation upon which beliefs are Influence of Culture and Upbringing:

Investigate how cultural and societal norms shape our beliefs from an early age, molding our worldview and influencing our values.

The Power of Conditioning: Examine the impact of conditioning on belief formation, as experiences and repeated patterns solidify our convictions, even in the absence of evidence.

Religion and Spirituality: We delve into the role of religion and spirituality as sources of belief, exploring the comfort, guidance, and sense of purpose they provide to individuals and communities.

Scientific Rationality: We contrast belief based on faith with belief founded on scientific evidence.

Emotional and Intuitive Beliefs: Uncover the significance of emotional and intuitive beliefs, which often defy logic but profoundly impact our perceptions and decisions.

Belief as a Coping Mechanism: Understand how belief serves as a coping mechanism during times of uncertainty and adversity, offering hope and comfort in challenging circumstances.

Formation of Core Beliefs: Explore the development of core beliefs, the deeply ingrained convictions that shape our self-identity and worldview.

The Role of Media and Information: Examine the influence of media and information sources on belief formation, and how misinformation and bias can shape collective beliefs.

Belief and Identity: Investigate the connection between belief and personal identity, as our convictions often become intertwined with how we define ourselves.

Belief and Social Identity Theory: Understand how our beliefs are influenced by our social identities and the need for belonging within groups.

Questioning Belief: Here we explore the importance of critical thinking and the process of questioning our own beliefs, fostering growth and personal evolution.

The Nature of Certainty and Doubt: Reflect on the nature of certainty and doubt, and how striking a balance between the two is essential for intellectual humility and open-mindedness.

As we venture into the realm of belief, we will unravel its complexities, recognizing that beliefs are not fixed entities but dynamic constructs that evolve over time. By beneficial the sources that underpin our convictions, we gain insight into the malleability of belief and the potential to shape our own perspectives. Let us journey deeper into the psyche, seeking to comprehend the driving forces behind our beliefs and the paths that lead to self-awareness and transformative growth.

CHAPTER 16
Defining Belief

Belief is a fundamental psychological and cognitive concept that goes beyond being a mere abstract idea. It is a mental state in which an individual holds a conviction or acceptance that something is true, real, or valid. Beliefs play a significant role in shaping how we perceive and interact with the world around us.

1. Conviction and Acceptance: At its core, belief involves having a strong conviction or acceptance of something, whether it's an idea, concept, value, or even a person. This conviction is often based on personal experiences, information, evidence, or cultural conditioning.

2. Power to Influence: Beliefs hold immense power over us because they shape our attitudes, behaviors, and decisions. They act as mental filters through which we interpret events and situations, determining how we respond to them.

3. Attitudes: Our beliefs influence the attitudes we adopt toward various aspects of life. For example, if someone believes that hard work leads to success, they are likely to approach challenges with determination and perseverance.

4. Behaviors: Beliefs also impact our behaviors. People tend to act in alignment with their beliefs, as their convictions drive their actions. For instance, if someone firmly believes in environmental conservation, they are more likely to adopt eco-friendly behaviors.

5. Decisions: Our beliefs heavily influence the choices we make in life. These can range from mundane decisions like what to wear or eat to major life choices such as career paths, relationships, and life goals.

6. Worldview Construction: Beliefs are building blocks that form our worldview. They create a lens through which we interpret reality, shaping our understanding of ourselves, others, and the broader universe.

7. Subjectivity and Diversity: Beliefs are highly subjective and vary significantly from person to person, culture to culture, and across different societies. What one person believes to be true may not align with another's beliefs.

8. Fluid Nature of Beliefs: Beliefs can change and evolve over time, influenced by new experiences, exposure to different perspectives, and updated information. This fluidity allows for personal growth and adaptation.

9. Confirmation Bias: Beliefs can be reinforced through a cognitive bias known as confirmation bias. This bias leads us to seek out information that supports our

existing beliefs while ignoring or dismissing evidence that contradicts them.

Understanding the nature of beliefs is crucial because they play a pivotal role in our thoughts, emotions, and actions. By becoming aware of our own beliefs and recognizing their influence, we can actively assess their validity, question assumptions, and choose beliefs that align with our values and aspirations. This self-awareness empowers us to shape our attitudes and behaviors consciously, leading to personal development and more meaningful engagement with the world around us.

CHAPTER 17
The Role of Perception

Perception and belief are intricately connected in shaping our understanding of the world. Perception refers to the process through which we interpret and make sense of the sensory information we receive from the environment. It involves the integration of sensory inputs such as sight, sound, taste, touch, and smell to construct a coherent and meaningful understanding of reality.

Perception acts as the lens through which we view the world, and it greatly influences the formation of our beliefs. Our interpretations of events, experiences, and information create the foundation upon which beliefs are built. For example, two individuals experiencing the same event may form different beliefs about it based on their unique perceptions of the situation.

The interplay between perception and belief can be complex and multifaceted. Our preexisting beliefs can shape how we perceive new information, a phenomenon known as belief bias. In other cases, our perceptions can reinforce or challenge existing beliefs, leading to a continuous feedback loop between the two.

Understanding the relationship between perception and belief is essential because it highlights the subjectivity of human experience. It reminds us that our beliefs are not objective truths but rather interpretations of reality influenced by our perceptions, past experiences, and cultural influences.

CHAPTER 18
Influence of Culture and Upbringing

Culture and upbringing are powerful forces that significantly shape our beliefs and worldview. Culture refers to the shared beliefs, values, customs, traditions, and behaviors of a particular group of people, often shaped by historical, geographical, and social factors. Upbringing, on the other hand, refers to the experiences, values, and beliefs instilled in individuals during their formative years, primarily by their family, caregivers, and community.

Both culture and upbringing act as influential agents in the belief formation process: Norms and Values: Culture and upbringing provide individuals with a set of norms and values that influence their moral compass and sense of right and wrong. They help shape attitudes toward issues such as family, relationships, authority, and societal roles.

CHAPTER 19
Religious Beliefs

Culture and upbringing can heavily influence religious beliefs and practices. People often adopt the predominant religious beliefs of their culture or follow the religious traditions of their family.

Language and Communication: Cultural and linguistic differences influence the way people communicate and perceive the world. Certain concepts or beliefs may not exist in one culture or may be interpreted differently.

Social Identity and Belonging: Cultural and familial ties contribute to an individual's sense of identity and belonging. Belonging to a particular cultural or social group can reinforce specific beliefs and values.

Traditions and Rituals: Cultural traditions and rituals, passed down through generations, play a role in belief reinforcement and cultural continuity.

Cultural Relativism: Cultural differences can lead to diverse beliefs and practices across societies, fostering an appreciation for cultural relativism—the understanding that beliefs should be understood within their cultural context.

CHAPTER 20
Challenging Beliefs

Exposure to different cultures and perspectives can challenge and expand an individual's beliefs, promoting cross-cultural understanding and empathy.

The influence of culture and upbringing on belief formation is significant and enduring. Recognizing this influence allows individuals to cultivate open-mindedness, embrace cultural diversity, and critically examine their own beliefs in the context of broader cultural influences. It also underscores the importance of promoting inclusive and respectful dialogue among people from different cultural backgrounds, from an early age, molding our worldview and influencing our values.

The Power of Conditioning: Conditioning refers to the process by which experiences, and repeated patterns influence our beliefs, attitudes, and behaviors over time. It is a fundamental aspect of human learning, where individuals make associations between stimuli and responses based on their experiences and interactions with the environment.

In the context of belief formation, conditioning plays a crucial role in shaping our convictions and perceptions of the world, even in the absence of concrete evidence. There are two primary forms of conditioning:

Classical Conditioning: This form of conditioning, famously studied by Ivan Pavlov, involves associating a neutral stimulus with an unconditioned stimulus to evoke a response. Over time, the neutral stimulus alone can elicit a similar response. For example, if a person repeatedly hears positive messages about a certain idea or product (neutral stimulus) while experiencing pleasure or positive emotions (unconditioned stimulus), they may develop a positive belief or attitude toward that idea or product.

Operant Conditioning: This type of conditioning, studied by B.F. Skinner, involves strengthening or weakening behavior through reinforcement or punishment. When a behavior is rewarded, it is more likely to be repeated, while punishment decreases the likelihood of that behavior occurring again. In the context of belief formation, positive reinforcement for holding certain beliefs can lead to their solidification, even if objective evidence is lacking.

The power of conditioning lies in its ability to create automatic associations and responses. Over time, repeated exposure to certain information, narratives, or experiences can shape our beliefs, even when we don't consciously recognize the influence. Conditioning can be seen in various aspects of life, including:

CHAPTER 21
Advertising and Marketing

Repeated exposure to advertisements can create positive associations with certain products or brands, influencing consumer beliefs and purchasing decisions.

Cultural and Social Norms: Social conditioning can shape beliefs about gender roles, societal expectations, and cultural values, impacting how individuals perceive themselves and others.

Political Beliefs: Exposure to specific political ideologies and narratives can condition individuals to adopt certain political beliefs without questioning their validity.

Prejudice and Bias: Conditioning can contribute to the development of prejudiced beliefs by associating negative stereotypes with certain groups, leading to discriminatory attitudes.

Recognizing the influence of conditioning on belief formation is essential for promoting critical thinking and open-mindedness. Understanding how beliefs can be shaped by conditioning allows individuals to approach information with a more discerning eye, questioning the sources of their convictions and seeking evidence-based reasoning. By fostering a habit of critical inquiry, individuals can better navigate the complex landscape of beliefs, forming more informed and rational perspectives.

CHAPTER 22
Religion and Spirituality

Religion and spirituality are significant sources of belief that have played a central role in human societies for millennia. They encompass systems of beliefs, practices, rituals, and values that offer individuals and communities a framework for understanding the meaning of life, the universe, and their place within it. Let's delve into their role as sources of belief and the various ways they provide comfort, guidance, and a sense of purpose to people and communities.

1. Comfort and Support: Religion and spirituality often provide a sense of comfort and solace to individuals, especially during times of distress or uncertainty. Believers may find reassurance in the belief that a higher power or force is watching over them and guiding them through challenging situations.

2. Community and Belonging: Religious and spiritual communities create a sense of belonging and social cohesion. They offer a shared belief system and a network of support, fostering a sense of community and unity among their members.

3. Moral and Ethical Guidance: Religion and spirituality

often provide moral and ethical guidelines for adherents to follow. They offer a framework for distinguishing between right and wrong, and many religious teachings emphasize compassion, kindness, and empathy towards others.

4. Meaning and Purpose: These belief systems address fundamental questions about the purpose of life, the nature of existence, and the afterlife. They provide individuals with a sense of purpose and direction, helping them find meaning in their experiences.

5. Rituals and Traditions: Religious and spiritual practices involve rituals, ceremonies, and traditions that provide a structured and symbolic way to connect with the divine or spiritual aspects of life. These rituals can foster a sense of connection and transcendence.

6. Sense of Identity: Religion and spirituality contribute to the formation of personal and cultural identities. They can shape an individual's worldview and influence their values, beliefs, and behaviors.

7. Coping with Grief and Loss: Beliefs about the afterlife and the continuity of the soul can offer comfort to individuals experiencing grief and loss, providing a framework for understanding life and death.

8. Exploring the Unseen: Spirituality often involves

exploring aspects of life beyond the tangible and material, such as consciousness, intuition, and interconnectedness with nature and the cosmos.

9. Encouraging Virtuous Lives: Many religious and spiritual beliefs promote virtuous behaviors and encourage adherents to strive for personal growth and self-improvement.

10. Source of Inspiration: Religion and spirituality have inspired some of humanity's greatest art, literature, music, and architecture, reflecting the profound impact of these beliefs on human creativity and cultural expression.It is essential to recognize that beliefs in religion and spirituality can be diverse and vary significantly across different cultures, traditions, and individuals. While they offer comfort, guidance, and purpose to many, they may not resonate with everyone, and some individuals may find meaning and belief through other philosophical or secular perspectives.

The study of religion and spirituality has also led to rich dialogues and debates on matters of faith, reason, and the nature of existence. Regardless of personal beliefs, understanding the role of religion and spirituality in human society helps foster tolerance, respect, and appreciation for the diversity of beliefs and worldviews that enrich the human experience.

CHAPTER 23
Scientific Rationality

Scientific rationality involves a systematic and evidence-based approach to understanding the world and making informed decisions. It contrasts belief based on faith with belief founded on scientific evidence. In this context, let's explore the role of reason and empirical evidence in shaping our convictions.

1. Faith-Based Belief: Faith-based belief relies on trust, conviction, or acceptance without the need for empirical evidence or logical reasoning. It often centers around matters that are beyond the scope of scientific investigation, such as religious doctrines, spiritual experiences, or supernatural phenomena. Faith is deeply personal and can be a source of comfort, guidance, and purpose for individuals, but it does not rely on empirical verification.

2. Scientific Evidence-Based Belief: Scientific beliefs are grounded in empirical evidence obtained through rigorous observation, experimentation, and peer-reviewed research. The scientific method involves formulating hypotheses, conducting experiments, and analyzing data to arrive at evidence-based conclusions. Scientific knowledge is dynamic and subject to revision

as new evidence emerges.

3. Role of Reason and Critical Thinking: Scientific rationality places a strong emphasis on reason and critical thinking. It encourages individuals to evaluate evidence objectively, question assumptions, and seek logical explanations for phenomena. Critical thinking helps to guard against biases and ensures that conclusions are based on the strength of the evidence.

4. Objectivity and Reproducibility: The scientific process aims for objectivity, meaning that findings are independent of personal beliefs or opinions. Scientific experiments and studies should be reproducible, allowing other researchers to verify or refute the results independently.

5. Testability and Falsifiability: Scientific hypotheses are testable and falsifiable, meaning that they can be subjected to empirical testing and potentially proven wrong. This principle ensures that scientific theories are open to scrutiny and refinement.

6. Empirical Verification: Scientific beliefs require empirical verification through systematic observation and experimentation. This process involves collecting data and conducting analyses to support or reject a hypothesis.

7. The Expanding Body of Knowledge: One of the strengths of scientific rationality is its ability to accumulate knowledge over time. New evidence and discoveries build upon existing scientific theories, leading to a deeper understanding of the natural world.

8. Consensus and Peer Review: Scientific findings undergo peer review, a process where experts in the field critically assess the quality and validity of research. Consensus among the scientific community strengthens the reliability of scientific beliefs.

9. Complementarity with Faith: Scientific rationality and faith-based belief can coexist for many individuals. While science addresses questions about the natural world, faith can provide answers to existential and spiritual questions beyond the scope of scientific investigation.

Balancing scientific rationality and faith is a personal choice, and many people find harmony between the two by recognizing that they address different aspects of life. While scientific evidence provides valuable insights into the natural world, faith can offer a deeper sense of purpose, connection, and existential meaning. Both perspectives contribute to the richness of human experience and understanding. Emphasizing the value of scientific rationality can lead to evidence-based decision-making and informed public discourse, promoting progress and well-being for society.

CHAPTER 24
Emotional and Intuitive Beliefs

Emotional and intuitive beliefs are a unique category of beliefs that are based on feelings, emotions, and gut instincts rather than on logical reasoning or empirical evidence. While traditional beliefs are often grounded in rational thought and empirical verification, emotional and intuitive beliefs emerge from a different cognitive process—one that relies on emotions, hunches, and subjective experiences.

1. Emotional Beliefs: Emotional beliefs stem from our emotions and feelings about a particular subject or situation. These beliefs are heavily influenced by our emotional experiences, past traumas, and positive or negative associations with certain ideas. Emotional beliefs can be powerful and enduring, as they are tied to our deeply ingrained emotional responses.

2. Intuitive Beliefs: Intuitive beliefs arise from a rapid, instinctive, and unconscious thought process. They often seem to come from "gut feelings" or a "sixth sense." Intuition can lead us to form beliefs or make decisions without being fully aware of the underlying reasons, making it difficult to articulate why we hold certain beliefs.

3. Defying Logic: Emotional and intuitive beliefs may defy conventional logic or lack objective evidence. They can coexist alongside rational beliefs and may even conflict with them. These beliefs can arise in situations where there is limited information, ambiguity, or complex emotions involved.

4. Impact on Perceptions: Emotional and intuitive beliefs can profoundly influence our perceptions and interpretations of reality. They shape how we perceive events, situations, and people, often leading us to see the world through the lens of our emotions and intuitions.

5. Role in Decision-Making: Emotional and intuitive beliefs can play a significant role in decision-making, especially in situations where time or information is limited. They can guide us toward certain choices, even if the logical reasoning may suggest otherwise.

6. Influence on Behavior: These beliefs can impact our behaviors and actions, sometimes leading us to act in ways that may not align with our rational thoughts. Emotional and intuitive beliefs can override logical considerations in influencing our actions.

7. Subjectivity and Personal Experience: Emotional and intuitive beliefs are highly subjective and are often influenced by individual experiences and personal history. Different people may hold contrasting

emotional and intuitive beliefs about the same subject.

8. Sources of Wisdom: While emotional and intuitive beliefs may not be based on objective evidence, they can sometimes tap into a deeper level of wisdom or insight. Many people value intuition as a source of guidance and creativity, especially in artistic and spiritual domains.

Understanding emotional and intuitive beliefs is essential because they can significantly impact our decisions, perceptions, and behaviors. While rational beliefs are critical for making well-informed choices, emotional and intuitive beliefs also hold value as they connect us with our emotions and intuitive senses. Finding a balance between rationality and emotional intuition allows us to approach complex situations with a broader perspective and make decisions that align with both our logical reasoning and our deeper emotional understanding.

CHAPTER 25
The Influence of Authority

Authority figures, whether in academia, politics, or other domains, possess significant influence over the beliefs of others. This influence stems from the perception of their expertise, credibility, and leadership, which often leads people to defer to their opinions and ideas. Understanding the impact of authority on belief formation is crucial because it can shape public opinion, individual attitudes, and even societal norms.

1. Perceived Expertise: Authority figures are often perceived as experts in their respective fields, possessing knowledge, experience, and qualifications that lend credibility to their statements. People tend to trust and believe individuals who are seen as knowledgeable and competent in specific areas.

2. Information Source: As authoritative sources of information, these figures play a crucial role in disseminating ideas and shaping public discourse. Their statements and opinions can reach a broad audience through media, speeches, publications, and other communication channels.

3. Social Influence: Authority figures hold positions

of power and influence within their communities, organizations, or societies. Their beliefs and decisions can set examples and norms for others, leading people to adopt similar beliefs or conform to prevailing ideologies.

4. Confirmation Bias: People may unconsciously seek out and give more weight to information that aligns with the beliefs of authority figures they admire or respect. This confirmation bias can reinforce existing beliefs and discourage critical thinking.

5. Power Dynamics: The power dynamics between authority figures and their followers can influence belief adoption. Followers may feel compelled to align their beliefs with those of the authority figure to maintain social harmony or avoid potential repercussions.

6. Emotional Appeal: Authority figures often use emotional appeals to influence beliefs. By leveraging emotions such as fear, hope, or compassion, they can shape public opinion and rally support for specific causes or ideas.

7. Leadership and Charisma: Charismatic authority figures can inspire strong emotional connections with their followers, creating a sense of loyalty and trust that enhances their influence over beliefs.

8. Public Perception and Media: The media plays a significant role in portraying authority figures, shaping public perception of their credibility and trustworthiness. Positive media coverage can amplify the influence of authority figures.

9. Challenge to Critical Thinking: Blindly accepting the beliefs of authority figures without critical examination can hinder independent thinking and foster intellectual dependence on others' ideas.

10. Ethical Responsibility: Authority figures have a responsibility to use their influence ethically and responsibly, promoting evidence-based information and avoiding the spread of misinformation or false beliefs. It is essential for individuals to exercise discernment and critical thinking when considering the beliefs and ideas propagated by authority figures. Relying solely on the authority of a person or position can lead to uncritical acceptance of potentially flawed or biased beliefs. Encouraging a culture of open dialogue, questioning, and evidence-based reasoning can help mitigate the undue influence of authority figures on belief formation, promoting a society that values diverse perspectives and informed decision-making.

CHAPTER 26
Belief as a Coping Mechanism

Belief, in various forms, can act as a powerful coping mechanism during times of uncertainty and adversity. When individuals encounter challenging circumstances or face situations that seem overwhelming, beliefs can provide comfort, hope, and a sense of control. Belief serves as an internal resource that people can tap into to navigate difficult emotions and find resilience in the face of adversity.

1. Providing Hope: Belief offers hope during trying times, creating a positive outlook and fostering optimism for the future. Believing in a better outcome or in the potential for personal growth can be a source of motivation and strength.

2. Sense of Control: Belief can provide a perceived sense of control over a situation. Even in circumstances beyond one's immediate control, believing in one's ability to cope or influence outcomes can reduce feelings of helplessness.

3. Reducing Anxiety: In times of uncertainty, belief can reduce anxiety by providing a sense of certainty or stability. Believing in higher powers, cosmic order, or fate can offer comfort by framing events as part of a

greater plan.

4. Emotional Regulation: Belief can assist in emotional regulation by providing a framework for processing and understanding emotions. Spiritual beliefs, for example, may offer a context for grief, loss, or suffering, allowing individuals to find solace and acceptance.

5. Strengthening Resilience: Belief can bolster resilience, enabling individuals to bounce back from setbacks and challenges. A belief in personal strength or the support of a higher power can reinforce the ability to adapt and recover.

6. Sense of Purpose: Belief provides a sense of purpose and meaning, even in the face of difficult circumstances. This sense of purpose can anchor individuals during tough times, guiding them towards actions aligned with their values and convictions.

7. Creating a Supportive Community: Beliefs can form the foundation of a supportive community during challenging times. Shared beliefs can foster connections and offer emotional support through collective understanding and empathy.

8. Fostering Hope and Creativity: Belief in possibilities beyond the current situation can inspire creative problem-solving and innovative thinking, leading to

the discovery of new solutions and opportunities.

9. Adaptive Coping Strategies: Different beliefs can offer diverse coping strategies. Some may find solace in mindfulness practices, prayer, or meditation, while others may draw strength from a belief in their inner resilience and ability to overcome obstacles.

It is important to note that while belief can serve as a valuable coping mechanism, it is not a substitute for seeking professional help or addressing underlying issues during times of significant distress. Coping with adversity involves a multifaceted approach that may include support from friends and family, seeking professional counseling, and employing various coping strategies.

Belief as a coping mechanism can be deeply personal and subjective, varying from person to person based on individual experiences, cultural backgrounds, and belief systems. Whether spiritual, philosophical, or personal, beliefs offer a source of comfort and hope, guiding individuals through the challenges that life presents.

CHAPTER 27
Formation of Core Beliefs

Explore the development of core beliefs, the deeply ingrained convictions that shape our self-identity and worldview.

The Role of Media and Information:

Media and information sources play a pivotal role in shaping belief formation, influencing individual perspectives, and shaping collective beliefs in society. With the advent of modern communication technologies, the media has become a powerful tool for disseminating information, news, and opinions to a global audience. This influence can have both positive and negative impacts on how people perceive the world and form their beliefs.

1. Information Dissemination: Media platforms, such as newspapers, television, radio, and the internet, serve as primary sources of information for many people. The way information is presented, curated, and emphasized by the media can shape public perception and beliefs about various topics.

2. Framing and Agenda-Setting: Media outlets have the power to frame news stories, highlighting certain aspects while downplaying others. The media's agenda-setting

ability can influence what topics are deemed important, ultimately shaping public attention and opinions on particular issues.

3. Confirmation Bias: People often seek out media sources that align with their preexisting beliefs and values, reinforcing their confirmation bias. This phenomenon can lead to echo chambers, where individuals are exposed to information that reaffirms their existing beliefs, making it challenging to consider alternative perspectives.

4. Misinformation and Disinformation: The spread of misinformation and disinformation can significantly impact belief formation. False or misleading information, intentionally or unintentionally disseminated by media sources, can mislead the public and shape beliefs based on inaccurate or distorted facts.

5. Polarization and Division: Biased reporting and the proliferation of sensationalized content can contribute to polarization in society. When media outlets present information in a divisive manner, it can lead to the formation of opposing belief camps, hindering constructive dialogue and understanding.

6. Influence of Social Media: Social media platforms have amplified the speed and reach of information

dissemination. Content shared on these platforms can go viral, shaping public opinion and beliefs rapidly.

7. Fact-Checking and Media Literacy: The prevalence of misinformation highlights the importance of media literacy and fact-checking. Individuals must critically evaluate information from different sources to discern credible information from false or biased content.

8. Role of Journalistic Ethics: The adherence to journalistic ethics, such as objectivity, fairness, and accuracy, is crucial in maintaining the credibility of media sources and fostering trust among audiences.

9. Role in Social Change: Media can also play a positive role in promoting social change and raising awareness about important issues. Thoughtful reporting and in-depth coverage can inform public debate and drive positive action.

Recognizing the influence of media and information sources on belief formation is essential for cultivating a well-informed and discerning society. Encouraging media literacy, critical thinking, and cross-source verification can empower individuals to navigate the vast amount of information available and form beliefs based on evidence and a broad range of perspectives. It is essential for media outlets to maintain a commitment to accurate and unbiased reporting to uphold their role as credible sources of information in shaping public opinion.

CHAPTER 28
Belief and Identity

Belief and personal identity are deeply interconnected, as our convictions often become integral components of how we define ourselves and our sense of self. Our beliefs shape our values, attitudes, and worldview, influencing not only how we perceive the world but also how we see ourselves within it. This intricate relationship between belief and identity has profound implications for our self-concept, behavior, and interactions with others.

1. Shaping Self-Concept: Beliefs play a central role in shaping our self-concept—the collection of beliefs, perceptions, and evaluations we hold about ourselves. Believing in our abilities, values, and aspirations can foster a positive self-image, while self-doubt or negative beliefs can lead to a diminished sense of self.

2. Values and Priorities: Our beliefs, especially our core beliefs, are closely linked to our values and priorities. What we believe to be true or meaningful often guides our decision-making and shapes the way we interact with others and the world around us.

3. Moral Identity: Beliefs about right and wrong, morality, and ethical principles are central to our moral identity—

the aspect of our identity tied to our sense of virtue and integrity. Our moral beliefs form the foundation of our ethical behavior and guide our sense of responsibility.

4. Group Affiliation: Beliefs can contribute to group affiliations and social identities. People often identify with communities, cultures, or movements that share similar beliefs, strengthening their sense of belonging and connection to others.

5. Cognitive Consistency: We tend to seek cognitive consistency, aligning our beliefs with our self-concept. This means that we are more likely to accept beliefs that align with our existing identity and reject beliefs that contradict it.

6. Emotional Attachment: Our emotional investment in certain beliefs can be strong, especially if these beliefs are tied to our sense of purpose, values, or cultural identity. Emotional attachment to beliefs can make it challenging to consider alternative viewpoints.

7. Identity Threat: Challenges to our beliefs can be perceived as threats to our identity. When our beliefs are deeply ingrained in our self-concept, encountering opposing views can evoke strong emotional reactions and resistance.

8. Evolving Identity: As individuals grow and change,

so can their beliefs and identity. Life experiences, education, exposure to new perspectives, and personal growth can lead to shifts in beliefs and the redefinition of one's identity.

9. Identity and Belongingness: The connection between belief and identity can foster a sense of belongingness within social or ideological groups that share similar beliefs. This sense of belonging can provide emotional support and validation.

Understanding the connection between belief and identity is essential for fostering empathy and respectful dialogue in diverse societies. Recognizing that beliefs are deeply tied to individual and collective identities allows us to approach discussions with sensitivity and open-mindedness. Encouraging self-reflection and embracing the complexity of beliefs can promote constructive conversations that facilitate personal growth and mutual understanding.

CHAPTER 29
Belief and Social Identity Theory

Social Identity Theory, proposed by psychologist Henri Tajfel, explores how individuals' self-concept and beliefs are influenced by their membership in social groups. According to this theory, people strive to maintain a positive social identity, which leads them to identify with particular groups and adopt the beliefs and values associated with those groups. Our beliefs, therefore, are shaped by our social identities, as we seek to align ourselves with the norms and values of the groups to which we belong.

1. Group Membership and Belief Adoption: When individuals identify with a particular social group—whether it's based on race, ethnicity, religion, nationality, political affiliation, or other characteristics—they tend to adopt the beliefs and attitudes that are prevalent within that group. Belongingness to a group strengthens the desire to conform to its norms and values.

2. In-Group Favoritism: Social Identity Theory suggests that people exhibit in-group favoritism, meaning they tend to view their own group more positively than out-groups. This favoritism can lead to a heightened commitment to the beliefs and values of their in-group.

3. Need for Belongingness: Belongingness is a fundamental human need, and social groups provide a sense of identity and belonging. To maintain positive self-esteem, individuals often internalize the beliefs of their groups and align their beliefs with those of the group.

4. Identity Salience: The salience of a particular social identity—how important it is to an individual at a given time—can influence which beliefs are activated and emphasized. When a particular social identity becomes more salient, the beliefs associated with that identity gain prominence.

5. Group Norms and Conformity: Social groups often have established norms and values that guide the behavior and beliefs of their members. Conformity to group norms can reinforce the adoption of specific beliefs.

6. Identity Threat and Belief Defense: When a person's social identity is threatened or challenged, they may engage in belief defense. This involves reinforcing and protecting the beliefs associated with their group to maintain a positive social identity.

7. Intergroup Conflict: Social Identity Theory can help explain intergroup conflicts, where different groups

hold opposing beliefs and values. These conflicts often arise from the need to differentiate and define one's group in contrast to others.

8. Stereotypes and Prejudice: Social Identity Theory is relevant to understanding stereotypes and prejudice. Stereotypes are often based on beliefs and attitudes associated with specific social groups, and they serve to maintain group boundaries.

Understanding the relationship between belief and Social Identity Theory can help us comprehend the dynamics of group behavior, intergroup relations, and the formation of collective beliefs. By recognizing how our social identities influence our beliefs, we can foster empathy, promote intergroup understanding, and work towards creating inclusive societies that respect diverse perspectives and values. Encouraging open dialogue and critical thinking about the beliefs we adopt can help us navigate the complexities of group influence and make more informed decisions about our beliefs.

CHAPTER 30
Questioning Belief

Questioning our beliefs is an essential aspect of critical thinking and personadl growth. It involves examining the foundations of our convictions, being open to alternative perspectives, and challenging assumptions. By engaging in this process, we foster intellectual curiosity, develop a deeper understanding of ourselves and the world, and create opportunities for personal evolution.

1. Avoiding Cognitive Bias: Questioning our beliefs helps us avoid cognitive biases, which are inherent mental shortcuts that can lead to errors in judgment and decision-making. By critically assessing our beliefs, we reduce the influence of biases and strive for more objective and rational thinking.

2. Promoting Intellectual Humility: Embracing the practice of questioning our beliefs encourages intellectual humility—the recognition that our knowledge is limited, and we may not have all the answers. This humility opens us up to learning from others and considering diverse perspectives.

3. Fostering Growth and Adaptability: As we question our beliefs, we become more open to change and personal

growth. Being willing to challenge long-held beliefs can lead to new insights, personal development, and adaptability in the face of new information.

4. Encouraging Empathy and Understanding: Questioning our beliefs helps us empathize with others' viewpoints and experiences. By considering alternative perspectives, we gain a more comprehensive understanding of complex issues and cultivate empathy for those with different beliefs.

5. Strengthening Logical Reasoning: The process of questioning beliefs requires us to apply logical reasoning and evidence-based thinking. It enhances our ability to construct sound arguments and make well-informed judgments.

6. Resolving Cognitive Dissonance: When our beliefs conflict with new information or experiences, we may experience cognitive dissonance—the discomfort of holding conflicting beliefs. Questioning our beliefs allows us to resolve this dissonance by either adjusting our beliefs or seeking additional information.

7. Enhancing Decision-Making: Questioning beliefs can lead to more thoughtful and informed decision-making. When we critically examine our beliefs and the potential consequences of our choices, we are better equipped to

make decisions aligned with our values and goals.

8. Building a Stronger Sense of Self: Engaging in the process of questioning beliefs helps us develop a deeper understanding of our values and principles. It enables us to align our beliefs with our authentic self, fostering a stronger sense of identity.

9. Encouraging Lifelong Learning: Embracing a questioning mindset promotes lifelong learning. It encourages us to seek new knowledge, explore diverse perspectives, and continuously challenge our assumptions.

10. Embracing Uncertainty: Questioning beliefs also involves embracing uncertainty and ambiguity. It acknowledges that not all questions have straightforward answers and that being comfortable with uncertainty is a part of intellectual growth.

Incorporating the practice of questioning beliefs into our lives empowers us to become more discerning thinkers, better decision-makers, and more empathetic individuals. It fosters an environment of intellectual curiosity and humility, enabling personal growth and fostering deeper connections with others. By continually challenging our beliefs, we embark on a journey of self-discovery, expanding our horizons, and evolving into more well-rounded and compassionate individuals.

CHAPTER 31
The Nature of Certainty and Doubt

Certainty and doubt represent two contrasting aspects of our beliefs and knowledge. Certainty refers to a firm conviction or confidence in the truth or validity of a belief or idea. Doubt, on the other hand, involves skepticism or uncertainty about the accuracy or completeness of our beliefs. Both certainty and doubt play significant roles in shaping our worldview and how we interact with the world around us.

1. Certainty and Confidence: Certainty can provide a sense of security and confidence in our beliefs. It gives us a strong foundation from which to make decisions and take action. Confidence in our knowledge can be empowering and can motivate us to pursue our goals with determination.

2. Limitations of Certainty: While certainty can be reassuring, it has its limitations. Unwavering certainty may lead to closed-mindedness, dogmatism, and resistance to new ideas. It can prevent us from considering alternative perspectives or recognizing the complexity of certain issues.

3. Humility and Open-Mindedness: Doubt, when

embraced with intellectual humility, encourages open-mindedness and a willingness to question our beliefs. It allows us to acknowledge that we don't have all the answers and that our understanding is limited.

4. Intellectual Curiosity: Doubt fuels intellectual curiosity by driving us to seek knowledge, explore new ideas, and engage with diverse perspectives. It motivates us to learn and grow, even in areas where we feel confident.

5. Embracing Uncertainty: The acknowledgment of doubt and uncertainty is an essential aspect of intellectual honesty. Embracing uncertainty means acknowledging that some questions may not have definitive answers and being comfortable with ambiguity.

6. Critical Thinking: Doubt is a foundational element of critical thinking. It prompts us to question evidence, examine arguments, and evaluate the validity of information before forming beliefs or making decisions.

7. Balancing Certainty and Doubt: Striking a balance between certainty and doubt is crucial for intellectual humility and openness. Being too certain may lead to intellectual rigidity, while excessive doubt may lead to indecision or a lack of confidence in our beliefs.

8. Continuous Learning and Growth: The interplay between certainty and doubt encourages continuous

learning and personal growth. Embracing doubt allows us to update our beliefs based on new information and experiences, fostering intellectual development.

9. Respecting Diverse Perspectives: Balancing certainty and doubt fosters respect for diverse perspectives. It allows us to engage in constructive dialogue, even with those who hold different beliefs, and promotes empathy and understanding.

10. Pragmatism and Adaptability: A balanced approach to certainty and doubt promotes pragmatism and adaptability. It enables us to adjust our beliefs and actions based on evidence and changing circumstances.

Recognizing the dual nature of certainty and doubt enables us to cultivate intellectual humility, open-mindedness, and a genuine pursuit of knowledge. Striking a balance between these two aspects allows us to remain confident in our beliefs when supported by evidence, while also acknowledging the potential for fallibility and the need for continuous learning. Intellectual growth and the ability to engage in meaningful conversations with others flourish when we embrace both certainty and doubt as essential components of our intellectual journey.

PART III
INTRODUCTION

Truth vs. Lies What Happens When Half of the Country
Believes that Truth is a Lie, and a Lie is Truth?

In part 3 we explore the implications of a society divided by conflicting beliefs about truth and lies. When a significant portion of the population subscribes to the idea that truth can be manipulated and lies can be accepted as truth, profound consequences can unfold for the fabric of democracy, social cohesion, and the pursuit of objective reality.

1. Erosion of Trust: When half of the country questions the validity of information and institutions, trust in media, government, and other authoritative sources can erode. This erosion can hinder effective governance and collective decision-making.

2. Polarization and Fragmentation: The divergence of beliefs about truth and lies can exacerbate polarization, leading to the formation of echo chambers and filter bubbles. People tend to surround themselves with like-minded individuals, reinforcing their beliefs and dismissing opposing viewpoints.

3. Disinformation and Misinformation: When lies gain equal footing with truth, the spread of disinformation and misinformation becomes rampant. False narratives can shape public opinion and undermine the ability to address critical issues based on objective data.

4. Challenges to Democracy: A democracy relies on the

informed choices of its citizens. When truth becomes subjective, making informed decisions based on factual information becomes challenging, weakening the foundations of democratic governance.

5. Erosion of Reality: The blurring of truth and lies can lead to a distorted perception of reality. This can make it difficult to address real-world problems and prioritize evidence-based solutions.

6. Erosion of Objective Standards: In a society where truth is contested, objective standards for evaluating information and determining facts can be undermined. The lack of commonly accepted criteria for truth assessment can create confusion and disarray.

7. Impact on Media and Journalism: When half of the population doubts the credibility of media and journalism, the role of the press as a watchdog and source of objective reporting can be compromised, weakening its ability to hold power accountable.

8. Polarized Societal Narratives: Conflicting beliefs about truth and lies can lead to the development of competing narratives within society. These narratives may be driven by ideological agendas rather than factual evidence, leading to division and animosity.

9. Challenges to Education: Education is essential for

critical thinking and discerning truth from falsehoods. When half of the country questions the importance of objective truth, it can hinder the effectiveness of education in developing analytical skills.

10. Upholding Democracy and Truth: To address these challenges, society must emphasize the importance of upholding democratic values, safeguarding truth, and promoting media literacy and critical thinking.

Encouraging open dialogue, fact-checking, and adherence to ethical reporting can help counter the spread of disinformation.

Addressing the consequences of half the country embracing conflicting beliefs about truth and lies requires collective effort and a commitment to democratic principles. Rebuilding trust in institutions, media, and democratic processes is crucial to fostering a cohesive and informed society. By recognizing the significance of objective truth and nurturing a culture that values transparency, accountability, and evidence-based decision-making, we can work towards a future where truth is a unifying force rather than a divisive one.

CHAPTER 32
Erosion of Trust

Trust is the foundation of a functioning society. When a significant portion of the population questions the validity of information and institutions, it can lead to an erosion of trust in key pillars of society, such as the media, government, and other authoritative sources. This erosion of trust can have several far-reaching consequences:

1. Impaired Credibility of Institutions: Institutions like the media and government rely on the trust of the public to carry out their functions effectively. When trust erodes, the credibility of these institutions is called into question, and their ability to inform the public and govern with legitimacy can be compromised.

2. Reduced Public Engagement: When people lose trust in institutions, they may disengage from the political process and public discourse. This can lead to apathy and reduced participation in civic activities, hindering the democratic process.

3. Polarization and Distrustful Attitudes: Erosion of trust can deepen existing divisions within society. People may become more skeptical of information that challenges their preexisting beliefs, leading to the reinforcement

of echo chambers and filter bubbles.

4. Misinformation Amplification: Without trust in reputable sources, misinformation and disinformation can gain traction more easily. People may turn to alternative sources that validate their beliefs, even if those sources lack factual accuracy.

5. Decline in Information Quality: Institutions that value their credibility strive to provide accurate and reliable information. When trust erodes, there may be less incentive for institutions to maintain rigorous standards of journalism and fact-checking.

6. Skepticism of Public Policy: Public policies and decisions made by government institutions may be met with skepticism and resistance if trust in those institutions is low. This can hinder the implementation of effective policies and the pursuit of collective goals.

7. Weakening Social Cohesion: Trust in institutions fosters social cohesion by promoting a shared belief in the efficacy of collective efforts. Erosion of trust can lead to a more fragmented and divided society, making it challenging to address common challenges collectively.

8. Impact on International Relations: The erosion of trust in government institutions can have repercussions

on international relations. It may affect diplomatic relations and the perception of a country's reliability as a partner in international agreements.

9. Diminished Media Influence: Media plays a crucial role in informing the public and holding power accountable. When trust in media diminishes, the influence and impact of responsible journalism may be undermined.

10. Difficult Decision-Making: A lack of trust in authoritative sources can create uncertainty and indecision in collective decision-making. When people question the validity of information, it becomes challenging to find common ground and make informed choices.

Addressing the erosion of trust requires concerted efforts to rebuild transparency, accountability, and ethical practices within institutions. Strengthening media literacy and promoting fact-based reporting can also help combat misinformation and restore confidence in the media. Fostering open dialogue, respectful engagement with diverse perspectives, and prioritizing the common good over partisan interests are essential steps towards rebuilding trust in institutions and ensuring effective governance and collective decision-making. Trust is a precious asset that must be nurtured to foster a cohesive and resilient society.

CHAPTER 33
Polarization and Fragmentation

Polarization refers to the increasing ideological distance between different groups or individuals with opposing beliefs. When beliefs about truth and lies diverge, it can exacerbate polarization within society, leading to the formation of echo chambers and filter bubbles. Here's how this process unfolds and its consequences:

1. Formation of Echo Chambers: An echo chamber is an environment where individuals are exposed only to information that reinforces their existing beliefs. When people surround themselves with like-minded individuals or consume media that aligns with their beliefs, they enter echo chambers. This phenomenon occurs when individuals seek confirmation of their viewpoints rather than exposure to diverse perspectives.

2. Reinforcement of Preexisting Beliefs: Within echo chambers, beliefs are reinforced and amplified. People are less likely to encounter viewpoints that challenge their existing beliefs, leading to the further solidification of their positions.

3. Dismissal of Opposing Viewpoints: Exposure to opposing viewpoints is limited in echo chambers, and when encountered, these perspectives are often dismissed or discredited. This dismissal can further entrench polarization and inhibit constructive dialogue.

4. Reduced Empathy and Understanding: Echo chambers can lead to a lack of empathy and understanding towards those with different beliefs. Stereotyping and caricaturing opposing viewpoints become more common, hindering open communication and collaboration.

5. Filter Bubbles in Digital Spaces: On digital platforms, algorithms can create filter bubbles, where users are presented with content that aligns with their previous interactions. This can narrow the range of information users are exposed to and reinforce existing beliefs.

6. Fragmentation of Social Discourse: Polarization and filter bubbles can lead to the fragmentation of social discourse. People may interact only with those who share their beliefs, leading to a lack of common ground and shared understanding.

7. Distrust and Division: Polarization can breed distrust between groups with different beliefs. This division can weaken social cohesion and hinder collaborative

efforts to address shared challenges.

8. Reinforcement of Biases: Echo chambers and filter bubbles can reinforce cognitive biases, such as confirmation bias, where individuals seek information that confirms their preexisting beliefs, and cognitive dissonance, where people reject information that contradicts their beliefs.

9. Challenges to Democratic Discourse: In a polarized society, constructive democratic discourse becomes challenging. The willingness to engage in civil dialogue and compromise may decrease, making it difficult to find common ground on policy issues.

10. Impact on Decision-Making: Polarization can impact decision-making processes, as policies may be driven more by ideological stances than by objective analysis and evidence-based approaches.

Addressing polarization and fragmentation requires efforts to foster empathy, dialogue, and a commitment to understanding diverse perspectives. Encouraging exposure to different viewpoints, promoting media literacy, and supporting independent journalism can help individuals escape echo chambers and filter bubbles. Building bridges of communication and finding common ground on shared values can facilitate constructive engagement and bridge divides. By nurturing a culture of open-mindedness, respect, and active listening, societies can work towards reducing polarization and fostering a more cohesive and inclusive environment for meaningful discourse and collective problem-solving.

CHAPTER 34
Disinformation and Misinformation

Disinformation and misinformation are two significant challenges that arise when lies gain equal footing with truth in society. Both involve the spread of false or misleading information, but they differ in their intent and dissemination. When disinformation and misinformation proliferate, they can have detrimental effects on public discourse, decision-making, and the pursuit of objective reality. Here's how they can impact society:

1. Disinformation vs. Misinformation: Disinformation refers to intentionally false or misleading information spread with the purpose of deceiving or manipulating the public. It often originates from actors with vested interests, such as governments, political groups, or malicious individuals. Misinformation, on the other hand, refers to false information shared without malicious intent, often due to misunderstanding or lack of verification.

2. Undermining Trust in Information Sources: When disinformation and misinformation spread unchecked, they can erode trust in information sources, including media, institutions, and experts. People may become skeptical of all information, making it challenging to

discern truth from falsehood.

3. Influence on Public Opinion: False narratives, whether intentional or not, can shape public opinion on critical issues. When misinformation gains traction, it can sway perceptions, leading to uninformed beliefs and decisions.

4. Hindering Evidence-Based Decision-Making: Disinformation and misinformation can obstruct evidence-based decision-making. Policies and actions may be based on false premises, leading to suboptimal outcomes.

5. Impact on Social Media: Social media platforms can become breeding grounds for the rapid spread of disinformation and misinformation due to the ease of sharing content. Algorithms can amplify false information, contributing to filter bubbles and echo chambers.

6. Polarization and Division: False information can fuel polarization by deepening existing divides. People may adopt extreme positions based on false narratives, further fragmenting society.

7. Public Health Concerns: Misinformation, especially in the context of public health, can be dangerous. False information about medical treatments or vaccines can lead to harmful consequences and exacerbate health crises.

8. Damage to Reputation and Trust: Disinformation campaigns can damage the reputation of individuals, organizations, or entire communities, leading to long-term consequences for trust and credibility.

9. Strain on Fact-Checking Resources: The proliferation of disinformation and misinformation places a strain on fact-checking organizations and independent journalists who work to verify information and combat falsehoods.

10. Challenges to Media Literacy: Misinformation can be difficult to detect, and individuals may inadvertently share false information. Promoting media literacy and critical thinking skills is crucial to equip people with tools to identify and combat misinformation.

Addressing disinformation and misinformation requires a multifaceted approach. Fact-checking efforts, media literacy programs, and responsible journalism can help combat the spread of false information. Social media platforms can implement measures to curb the rapid dissemination of misinformation. Encouraging individuals to verify information before sharing it and fostering a culture that values truth and accuracy in public discourse can collectively contribute to countering the detrimental impact of disinformation and misinformation on society. By prioritizing the importance of truth and accuracy in information dissemination, we can protect the integrity of public discourse and decision-making processes, fostering a more informed, cohesive, and resilient society.

CHAPTER 35
Challenges to Democracy

Democracy is built on the fundamental principle of informed decision-making by its citizens. When truth becomes subjective and the objective nature of facts is questioned, several challenges arise that can weaken the foundations of democratic governance:

1. Misinformed Electorate: In a democracy, citizens vote to elect representatives and make important decisions through referendums and initiatives. When false or misleading information spreads, it can lead to a misinformed electorate, making it difficult for people to make well-informed choices.

2. Manipulation of Public Opinion: Disinformation campaigns can manipulate public opinion, influencing voting behaviors and policy preferences. When false narratives gain traction, they can sway perceptions and attitudes, leading to decisions that may not align with the best interests of society.

3. Polarization and Gridlock: When citizens are exposed to conflicting information, it can deepen existing divisions and create gridlock in decision-making processes. The inability to reach consensus or common ground on

issues can hinder progress and effective governance.

4. Erosion of Trust in Institutions: Democracy relies on the trust of its citizens in institutions, such as the government, media, and judiciary. When truth becomes subjective, trust in these institutions may erode, impacting their ability to govern effectively and address societal challenges.

5. Distrust in Elections: Disinformation about the integrity of elections can undermine public trust in the electoral process. If citizens doubt the fairness and legitimacy of elections, it can lead to reduced voter turnout and skepticism about election outcomes.

6. Manipulation of Political Discourse: Disinformation campaigns can manipulate political discourse by introducing false narratives into public debates. This can divert attention from substantive issues and create a toxic environment of misinformation and mistrust.

7. Decline in Civic Engagement: When citizens are bombarded with false or misleading information, they may become disillusioned and disengaged from the political process. This decline in civic engagement can weaken democracy's ability to reflect the will of the people.

8. Influence of Special Interests: Disinformation can be

strategically employed by special interest groups to further their own agendas. When truth is obscured, these groups may gain disproportionate influence over policy decisions.

9. Undermining Democratic Values: The prevalence of disinformation challenges core democratic values, such as transparency, accountability, and the free exchange of ideas. It can lead to an erosion of these values and weaken democratic norms.

10. Threat to Media Freedom: Disinformation can be used to discredit media organizations and undermine their independence. This poses a threat to media freedom, an essential component of a healthy democracy.

Addressing challenges to democracy requires a commitment to promoting media literacy, critical thinking, and fact-based reporting. Fact-checking efforts, transparency in information dissemination, and accountability for the spread of false information are essential to protect democratic processes. Encouraging an informed and engaged citizenry is vital for upholding democratic values and ensuring that decisions are made based on accurate information. By safeguarding the integrity of information and fostering a culture that values truth and accountability, we can strengthen the foundations of democratic governance and ensure that democracy continues to be a system that serves the collective interests of its citizens.

Chapter 36

Erosion of Reality

When truth and lies become blurred, it can lead to an erosion of reality, where a distorted perception of facts and events prevails. This distortion can have significant consequences, making it challenging to address real-world problems and prioritize evidence-based solutions. Here's how the erosion of reality can impact society:

1. Loss of Common Ground: In a society where truth is contested, finding common ground becomes difficult. People may hold divergent views on basic facts, hindering constructive dialogue and collaboration on pressing issues.

2. Conflicting Narratives: The blurring of truth and lies can lead to the emergence of multiple conflicting narratives about events and phenomena. This can create confusion and division among the public.

3. Obstruction of Evidence-Based Decision-Making: Evidence-based decision-making relies on objective facts and data. When reality is eroded by the prevalence of false information, it becomes challenging to make well-informed policy decisions.

4. Inefficiency in Problem-Solving: Addressing real-world problems requires an accurate understanding of their root causes. The erosion of reality can impede the identification of these causes, leading to less effective problem-solving efforts.

5. Polarization and Partisanship: When reality is contested, people may gravitate towards narratives that align with their preexisting beliefs. This can deepen polarization and entrench partisanship, making it difficult to reach consensus on policy matters.

6. Disregard for Expertise: The erosion of reality can lead to a disregard for expertise and evidence-based analysis. People may dismiss expert opinions and scientific findings, further complicating efforts to address complex challenges.

7. Spread of Conspiracy Theories: When reality is eroded, conspiracy theories and unfounded claims can gain popularity. These beliefs can have harmful effects on public discourse and decision-making.

8. Impacts on Public Health: In the context of public health, the erosion of reality can be especially damaging. Misinformation about health issues can lead to behaviors that exacerbate health crises.

9. Weakening Trust in Institutions: A distorted perception

of reality can weaken trust in institutions and media, leading to skepticism about the information they provide.

10. Threat to Democracy: An erosion of reality poses a threat to democratic governance, as decisions may be made based on unfounded beliefs rather than factual information.

Addressing the erosion of reality requires a commitment to promoting accurate and evidence-based information. Fact-checking efforts, media literacy programs, and critical thinking education can help individuals discern fact from fiction. Responsible journalism and transparency in information dissemination are crucial for countering the spread of false information. Engaging in open and constructive dialogue that is grounded in facts and evidence can help bridge divides and build consensus on pressing issues. By actively upholding the importance of objective truth and fostering a culture that values evidence-based decision-making, society can mitigate the erosion of reality and pave the way for more effective problem-solving and progress.

CHAPTER 37
Erosion of Objective Standards

Objective standards are essential for evaluating information, determining facts, and establishing a shared understanding of reality within society. In a society where truth is contested and the distinction between truth and falsehood becomes blurred, the erosion of objective standards can occur. This erosion can have significant consequences, leading to confusion, disarray, and a breakdown of consensus on truth. Here's how it impacts society:

1. Lack of Consensus on Truth: Objective standards serve as a basis for consensus on truth. When these standards are eroded, people may disagree on what constitutes reliable information and facts, making it difficult to establish shared truths.

2. Spread of Conflicting Information: Without commonly accepted criteria for truth assessment, conflicting information may circulate freely. Different sources may present divergent narratives, contributing to information overload and uncertainty.

3. Discrediting of Expertise: Objective standards are integral to recognizing and respecting expertise in

various fields. In the absence of such standards, expert opinions may be questioned, leading to the devaluation of specialized knowledge.

4. Difficulty in Decision-Making: Decision-making processes rely on accurate information. When objective standards are undermined, it becomes challenging to identify reliable data and evidence, hindering effective decision-making.

5. Impact on Policy Development: Objective standards provide a framework for evidence-based policy development. Their erosion can lead to the formulation of policies based on unsubstantiated claims or ideological biases.

6. Influence of Disinformation Campaigns: The erosion of objective standards creates fertile ground for disinformation campaigns. Without clear criteria for truth assessment, false information may gain equal footing with verified facts.

7. Polarization and Fragmentation: The lack of commonly accepted criteria for truth assessment can deepen existing divisions within society. People may gravitate towards sources that confirm their beliefs, reinforcing polarization.

8. Distrust in Institutions: Objective standards are

foundational to the credibility of institutions and media. The erosion of these standards can lead to distrust in these entities and a loss of faith in their ability to provide accurate information.

9. Vulnerability to Manipulation: In the absence of objective standards, people may be more susceptible to manipulation by those seeking to exploit the lack of clear criteria for truth assessment.

10. Challenges to Education: Objective standards are vital in education, guiding students in evaluating information critically. Their erosion can hinder the development of critical thinking skills and media literacy.

Addressing the erosion of objective standards requires a collective effort to uphold the importance of evidence-based thinking, critical analysis, and media literacy. Encouraging the use of reliable sources, fact-checking, and independent verification can help individuals discern credible information from misinformation. Promoting transparency in information dissemination and holding those who spread disinformation accountable are essential steps in restoring trust in objective standards. By reaffirming the value of evidence, reason, and objective truth, society can work towards reestablishing common ground and fostering a more informed, cohesive, and resilient community.

CHAPTER 38
Impact on Media and Journalism

A thriving democracy relies on a free and independent media that serves as a watchdog, providing objective reporting and holding those in power accountable. When a significant portion of the population doubts the credibility of media and journalism, it can have several adverse effects on the media's role and function within society. Here's how this impact unfolds:

1. Erosion of Trust: Doubts about media credibility erode public trust in news organizations. When people question the reliability of media sources, they may be less inclined to believe and rely on the information provided.

2. Polarization of Media Consumption: People may seek out media outlets that align with their preexisting beliefs, leading to the formation of echo chambers and filter bubbles. This polarization can deepen divisions within society.

3. Discrediting Objective Reporting: Media outlets strive to provide objective reporting based on verified information. When credibility is questioned, the perception of media bias may increase, undermining

the objectivity of reporting.

4. Influence of Disinformation: Disinformation campaigns can exploit doubts about media credibility, further muddying the waters of public discourse. False information may be disseminated, leading to confusion and misinformation.

5. Weakening of the Fourth Estate: A robust and independent media is often referred to as the Fourth Estate, acting as a check on government and other powerful institutions. Doubts about media credibility can weaken this essential role.

6. Challenges in Holding Power Accountable: Media serves as a crucial check on those in power, investigating and exposing potential abuses of authority. When media credibility is in question, its ability to hold power accountable may be compromised.

7. their ability to report freely.

8. Disengagement from News Consumption: When credibility is in question, some individuals may disengage from news consumption altogether, leading to a lack of information on critical issues.

Addressing the impact on media and journalism requires a commitment to upholding journalistic ethics, transparency, and accountability. Media organizations must redouble efforts to verify information, avoid sensationalism, and maintain independence from political or commercial pressures. Building media literacy among the public can empower individuals to critically evaluate news sources and discern reliable information. Efforts to combat disinformation and promote fact-checking are essential to restoring trust in journalism. By supporting a diverse and vibrant media landscape and recognizing the vital role of journalism in democracy, society can bolster the media's ability to fulfill its watchdog function and hold power accountable.

CHAPTER 39
Polarized Societal Narratives

When conflicting beliefs about truth and lies emerge within society, they can give rise to polarized narratives. These narratives represent divergent perspectives and interpretations of reality, often driven by ideological agendas rather than objective evidence. The development of polarized societal narratives can have significant consequences, leading to division, animosity, and a breakdown in shared understanding. Here's how this phenomenon impacts society:

1. Fragmentation of Society: Polarized narratives create divisions within society, as individuals and groups align themselves with different belief systems. This fragmentation can lead to a lack of common ground and shared values.

2. Echo Chambers and Filter Bubbles: People may seek out information and sources that confirm their preexisting beliefs, leading to the reinforcement of their perspectives within echo chambers and filter bubbles.

3. Escalation of Tensions: When polarized narratives clash, tensions can escalate, leading to animosity and conflict between different factions within society.

4. Difficulty in Constructive Dialogue: Constructive dialogue relies on a shared understanding of facts and evidence. Polarized narratives make it challenging to engage in meaningful conversations and find common solutions to societal challenges.

5. Weakening of Social Cohesion: Polarized narratives erode social cohesion, as individuals identify more strongly with their ideological groups than with the larger community.

6. Influence on Policy-Making: Polarized narratives can impact policy-making processes, as decisions may be driven more by ideological stances than by objective analysis and evidence-based approaches.

7. Skepticism of Opposing Views: In a polarized environment, people may be more inclined to dismiss opposing viewpoints without critically evaluating their merit, further entrenching divisions.

8. Misrepresentation of Facts: Polarized narratives may cherry-pick or misrepresent facts to support particular ideological positions, leading to misinformation and a distortion of reality.

9. Impact on Media Landscape: The prevalence of polarized narratives can influence media reporting, with outlets catering to specific ideological audiences,

reinforcing polarization.

10. Challenges to Democracy: A cohesive and informed citizenry is essential for the functioning of democracy. Polarized narratives can hinder informed decision-making and weaken the requires efforts to foster open dialogue, critical thinking, and media literacy. Promoting exposure to diverse perspectives and encouraging empathy and understanding can help bridge divides. Emphasizing evidence-based decision-making and encouraging fact-checking can counter the spread of misinformation and polarized narratives. Building trust in objective information and promoting a culture of respectful engagement can help reestablish common ground and foster a more cohesive and inclusive society. By recognizing the dangers of polarized narratives and working towards a more unified understanding of reality, societies can mitigate divisions and cultivate an environment that values evidence, reason, and constructive dialogue.

CHAPTER 40
Challenges to Education

Education plays a crucial role in nurturing critical thinking skills, promoting informed decision-making, and fostering a society that values evidence-based reasoning. When a significant portion of the country questions the importance of objective truth, it can present several challenges to education and hinder the development of analytical skills among students. Here's how this phenomenon impacts education:

1. Undermining the Importance of Facts: Education aims to equip students with factual knowledge and the ability to distinguish between facts and opinions. When objective truth is questioned, the importance of factual information may be undermined, leading to a disregard for evidence-based learning.

2. Impact on Critical Thinking: Critical thinking relies on the ability to analyze information, assess evidence, and make informed judgments. Doubts about objective truth can hinder the cultivation of critical thinking skills, leading to a less informed and engaged citizenry.

3. Erosion of Trust in Education Institutions: Education institutions are essential in promoting rigorous

academic standards and instilling a commitment to intellectual honesty. When objective truth is contested, trust in education institutions may decline, affecting the credibility of educational content.

4. Influence on Curriculum: Doubts about objective truth can influence educational curricula, leading to the inclusion of biased or ideologically driven content. This can distort the presentation of historical events or scientific principles.

5. Challenges in Teaching Controversial Topics: When objective truth is questioned, teaching controversial topics may become more challenging. Teachers may encounter resistance or skepticism from students or parents regarding established facts and evidence.

6. Impact on Media Literacy Education: Media literacy education aims to help students critically evaluate information sources. Doubts about objective truth can complicate media literacy instruction, as students may struggle to distinguish reliable sources from unreliable ones.

7. Rise of Misinformation Among Students: Students exposed to conflicting narratives about truth and falsehood may be more susceptible to misinformation. This can hinder their ability to engage in informed

discourse and contribute to a misinformed society.

8. Influence of Ideological Bias: Doubts about objective truth can lead to the promotion of ideological bias in educational materials. This can create an unbalanced view of historical events or scientific principles, hindering students' understanding of complex issues.

9. Disincentive for Pursuing Higher Education: When objective truth is contested, students may question the value of higher education and academic pursuits, leading to a decline in interest in pursuing advanced studies.

10. Impact on Future Decision-Makers: Education shapes future leaders and decision-makers. Doubts about objective truth can impact their ability to make evidence-based decisions, affecting policy-making and problem-solving in the future.

Addressing challenges to education requires a commitment to promoting evidence-based learning, critical thinking, and media literacy. Education institutions should uphold the importance of objective truth and maintain high academic standards. Integrating media literacy education into the curriculum can empower students to navigate the complex information landscape effectively. Encouraging open dialogue and fostering a culture that values evidence and reason are essential in countering the erosion of trust in education and developing analytical skills among students. By recognizing the significance of objective truth in education, societies can nurture an informed and engaged citizenry, capable of navigating the complexities of the modern world.

CHAPTER 41
Upholding Democracy and Truth

Addressing the challenges posed by the erosion of truth and the impact of disinformation requires a concerted effort from society as a whole. Upholding democratic values, safeguarding truth, and promoting media literacy and critical thinking are crucial steps in countering the spread of misinformation and ensuring a well-informed, engaged, and cohesive society. Here's how these measures can help:

1. Promoting Democratic Values: Reaffirming democratic values, such as freedom of speech, transparency, and accountability, is essential for fostering a culture that values truth and objective information. These values provide the foundation for an open and informed society.

2. Safeguarding Objective Truth: Recognizing the importance of objective truth and evidence-based thinking is essential for addressing challenges to truth and the erosion of reality. Valuing truth as a societal norm can help counter the spread of falsehoods and misinformation.

3. Media Literacy and Critical Thinking Education:

Introducing media literacy and critical thinking education in schools and communities can empower individuals to evaluate information critically, discern reliable sources, and identify misinformation.

4. Encouraging Fact-Checking and Verification: Fact-checking initiatives play a crucial role in countering disinformation. Encouraging individuals to fact-check information before sharing it can help prevent the spread of false narratives.

5. Responsible Reporting and Ethical Journalism: Media outlets must adhere to ethical reporting standards and prioritize accuracy, transparency, and unbiased reporting. Responsible journalism is vital in countering the spread of disinformation.

6. Open Dialogue and Constructive Discourse: Encouraging open dialogue and respectful engagement can foster understanding and bridge divides. Constructive discourse allows for the exchange of diverse perspectives and informed debates.

7. Collaboration with Tech Companies: Collaboration between tech companies and experts in combating disinformation can lead to the development of effective strategies for identifying and addressing false information online.

8. Support for Independent Fact-Checking Organizations: Supporting independent fact-checking organizations can strengthen their efforts in verifying information and providing accurate assessments of claims.

9. Strengthening Media Diversity: Promoting media diversity can counter the formation of echo chambers and filter bubbles. A diverse media landscape allows for a range of perspectives and viewpoints to be represented.

10. Empowering Informed Citizenship: Empowering citizens with accurate information and the tools to critically assess information is crucial for upholding democracy. Informed citizens are better equipped to engage in the democratic process and make well-informed decisions.

By emphasizing democratic values, promoting media literacy, and encouraging critical thinking, society can work towards countering the challenges posed by the erosion of truth and the spread of disinformation. Upholding truth as a shared value and fostering a commitment to evidence-based reasoning can help build a more resilient, cohesive, and informed community. Together, these efforts contribute to strengthening democracy and ensuring that truth remains a guiding principle in public discourse and decision-making processes.

PART IV
INTRODUCTION
Voting Rights And Human Rights Beliefs
The Threat To Democracy

When a certain segment of the country believes that certain groups, such as black people, people of color, and women, do not deserve the right to vote and they begin to strip away their voting rights and human rights, it poses a significant threat to democracy. Here's how this scenario can impact democracy:

1. Undermining Democratic Principles: Democracy is built on the principles of equality, inclusivity, and representation. When a segment of the population seeks to disenfranchise certain groups based on race or gender, it undermines these fundamental democratic principles.

In a healthy democracy, every citizen should have an equal and meaningful opportunity to participate in the decision-making processes that shape their society. The belief that certain groups, such as black people, people of color, and women, do not deserve the right to vote contradicts the very essence of democracy. Such beliefs perpetuate a system that is exclusive and discriminates against specific segments of the population, eroding the fundamental ideals upon which democratic societies are built.

Disenfranchising any group based on race or gender not only contradicts democratic principles but also runs counter to the principles of human rights and social justice.

It perpetuates historical patterns of discrimination and marginalization, which were fought against through the hard-fought battles of the civil rights movement and other human rights struggles.

Furthermore, when certain groups are excluded from the democratic process, the resulting governance lacks a genuine representation of the diverse perspectives and interests of the entire population. This undermines the very essence of representative democracy, where elected officials are supposed to be accountable to all citizens, not just a select few.

The denial of voting rights to certain groups also hampers progress towards a more inclusive and equitable society. Equal opportunity and social mobility, cornerstones of democratic values, become elusive when some members of society are systematically silenced and denied the right to participate in shaping their future.

To safeguard democratic principles, it is imperative to recognize the importance of protecting voting rights and human rights of all individuals, irrespective of their race, gender, ethnicity, or any other characteristic. Upholding the principles of democracy requires actively working towards breaking down barriers to participation, combating voter suppression efforts, and fostering a culture of inclusivity and equality.

Addressing historical injustices and promoting policies that promote equal access to education, economic opportunities, and political representation are essential in ensuring that every citizen's voice is heard and respected. By embracing diversity, striving for social cohesion, and standing firmly against any form of discrimination, societies can uphold democratic values and build a more robust and equitable democratic system for all. Only through a collective commitment to these democratic principles can societies forge a path towards a brighter, fairer, and more inclusive future.

2. Disenfranchisement and Marginalization: Stripping away voting rights from specific groups perpetuates historical patterns of disenfranchisement and marginalization. It can lead to the exclusion of these communities from the democratic process, limiting their ability to have a say in governance and policymaking.

Historically, disenfranchisement and marginalization have been used as tools of oppression to suppress the voices of certain communities and maintain existing power structures. When voting rights are stripped away from specific groups based on race, ethnicity, gender, or other characteristics, it perpetuates a troubling legacy of exclusion and inequality. These patterns of disenfranchisement hark back to a time when individuals were denied their basic human right to participate in the democratic process and shape the policies that directly impact their lives.

Disenfranchisement effectively silences the concerns, needs, and aspirations of these marginalized communities. It denies them the opportunity to elect representatives who genuinely understand and advocate for their interests, leading to a lack of meaningful representation in government and policymaking bodies. As a result, the voices of these communities are overshadowed, and their issues are often neglected, perpetuating a cycle of marginalization and underrepresentation.

Moreover, disenfranchisement has far-reaching consequences beyond the political sphere. It can exacerbate social and economic disparities, hindering the progress of these communities towards achieving equal opportunities and justice. When citizens are denied their right to vote, they lose a critical avenue for advocating for positive change and influencing the decisions that affect their access to education, healthcare, housing, and employment opportunities.

Disenfranchisement can also erode trust in institutions and the democratic process. When communities consistently experience barriers to voting and face obstacles in exercising their rights, it fosters a sense of alienation and disillusionment with the system. This can lead to a decline in civic engagement and further marginalize these communities from the broader societal fabric.

To address disenfranchisement and marginalization, societies must confront the historical legacies of discrimination and actively work towards dismantling barriers that prevent equal access to voting. Encouraging voter registration, implementing fair redistricting practices, expanding early voting options, and combatting voter suppression tactics are crucial steps in ensuring that all citizens can fully participate in the democratic process.

Additionally, promoting civic education and engagement in schools and communities can empower individuals with the knowledge and tools to advocate for their rights and actively participate in shaping their future. Advocating for policies that promote inclusivity, diversity, and equal representation in political leadership can also contribute to breaking down the barriers of disenfranchisement and fostering a more equitable and just democracy.

By confronting the historical injustices of disenfranchisement and actively working towards a more inclusive and participatory democratic system, societies can move closer to realizing the democratic ideal of providing equal representation and opportunity for all its citizens, irrespective of their background or identity. Only through concerted efforts to overcome marginalization and empower disenfranchised communities can democracy truly thrive as a force for positive change and progress.

3. Erosion of Trust in the Democratic System: When a segment of the population seeks to suppress the voting rights of specific groups, it erodes trust in the democratic system. People may question the legitimacy and fairness of the electoral process.

Trust is the cornerstone of any functioning democratic system. It is the belief that the electoral process is fair, impartial, and truly represents the will of the people. When a segment of the population actively seeks to suppress the voting rights of specific groups, it undermines this trust and casts doubt on the legitimacy of the entire democratic process.

The erosion of trust in the democratic system occurs on multiple levels:

1. Perceived Bias and Unfairness: When efforts are made to disenfranchise certain communities, it creates a perception of bias and unfairness in the electoral process. This perception can lead to a sense of disillusionment among affected communities and foster skepticism about the integrity of elections.

2. Questioning Election Outcomes: Suppression of voting rights may lead to questioning the legitimacy of election

outcomes. If certain groups are systematically denied their right to vote, election results may not accurately reflect the true preferences of the electorate.

3. Disenchantment with Political Institutions: Disenfranchisement efforts can lead to disillusionment with political institutions and the belief that the system is rigged to favor certain interests over others. This disenchantment can result in decreased civic engagement and a reduced willingness to participate in the democratic process.

4. Perception of Inequality: The denial of voting rights can reinforce the perception of inequality in society. When certain groups are systematically excluded from the democratic process, it reinforces a hierarchy of power that favors the privileged few over the marginalized many.

5. Impact on Voter Turnout: Suppression tactics, such as restrictive voter ID laws or voter purges, can deter eligible voters from participating in elections. This decline in voter turnout not only weakens democratic representation but also signals a lack of confidence in the system's ability to protect voting rights.

6. Weakening of Democratic Norms: Trust is critical for upholding democratic norms, such as accepting

election results and peacefully transitioning power. Erosion of trust in the democratic system can lead to increased political polarization and challenges to the peaceful transfer of power.

7. Polarization and Social Cohesion: When trust in the democratic system is undermined, it can exacerbate social divisions and polarize society. A lack of confidence in the fairness of elections can lead to increased animosity between different segments of the population.

Addressing the erosion of trust in the democratic system requires safeguarding the right to vote and ensuring that the electoral process remains accessible, inclusive, and free from discrimination. Implementing measures that promote voter registration, expand early voting options, and combat voter suppression tactics are vital steps to restore confidence in the electoral process.

Furthermore, transparency in the administration of elections, impartial redistricting, and the elimination of barriers to voting are crucial for instilling trust in the democratic system. Building a culture of civic engagement and promoting political education can also empower citizens to actively participate in the democratic process and hold elected officials accountable.

Ultimately, restoring trust in the democratic system requires a collective commitment to upholding democratic values, protecting voting rights, and ensuring that every voice is heard and respected in the political process. By nurturing a democracy that is truly representative, equitable, and responsive to the needs of all its citizens, societies can foster a sense of ownership and pride in their democratic institutions, strengthening the bonds that hold them together and advancing the principles of justice and equality for all.

4. Threat to Human Rights: Voting rights are an essential component of human rights, as they empower individuals to participate in decision-making that affects their lives. Stripping away these rights infringes upon the basic principles of human rights and dignity.

Human rights are universal entitlements that inherently belong to every individual, regardless of their background, race, gender, religion, or any other characteristic. Among these rights is the fundamental right to participate in the governance of one's society through the democratic process, and voting rights lie at the heart of this crucial human right.

Voting is not just a privilege; it is a fundamental expression of human agency, dignity, and autonomy. It is the mechanism through which individuals can shape the social, economic, and political policies that directly impact their lives, families, and communities. Stripping away voting rights from specific groups based on discriminatory beliefs or practices infringes upon these fundamental principles of human rights.

When voting rights are denied to certain segments of the population, it denies them the ability to participate fully in civic life, access equal opportunities, and contribute to the collective decision-making that defines their society. This denial perpetuates a cycle of marginalization and disempowerment, effectively relegating these communities to the margins of society.

Moreover, voting rights are closely tied to other human rights. Access to education, healthcare, employment opportunities, and social services often depends on the decisions made by elected officials. When individuals are excluded from the voting process, their ability to advocate for their rights and influence policies that affect them is severely curtailed.

Denying voting rights based on discriminatory beliefs also sends a deeply troubling message about the value and dignity of certain individuals or communities. It reinforces the notion that some groups are lesser and not entitled to full participation in the society they call home. This devaluation of human worth contradicts the very essence of human rights, which asserts the inherent dignity and equal worth of every person.

To uphold human rights, societies must recognize voting rights as an indispensable aspect of human dignity and social equality. Protecting and promoting voting rights for all citizens, irrespective of their background, is essential for building a just and inclusive society.

Addressing this threat to human rights requires confronting historical injustices, dismantling barriers to voting, and implementing policies that promote equal representation and participation in the democratic process. Ensuring free and fair elections, combating voter suppression tactics, and fostering a culture that values the human rights of every individual are essential steps in safeguarding the integrity and dignity of the democratic system.

By actively working towards protecting voting rights and promoting the principles of human dignity and equality, societies can uphold the spirit of human rights and build a democracy that truly reflects the collective will and aspirations of all its citizens. Only through this commitment to human rights can societies fulfill their duty to protect and empower every individual, creating a more just, compassionate, and equitable world for generations to come.

5. Polarization and Division:

Disenfranchisement efforts based on race or gender can deepen divisions within society, leading to increased polarization and animosity between different groups.

Disenfranchisement efforts, particularly those targeting specific racial or gender groups, can have a profoundly divisive impact on society. When certain segments of the population are deliberately excluded from the democratic process, it fosters a sense of exclusion and marginalization, intensifying existing divisions and creating new fault lines within society.

1. Heightened Identity Politics: Disenfranchisement based on race or gender can fuel identity politics, wherein individuals' political choices and loyalties become primarily defined by their racial or gender identity. This can lead to the formation of rigid blocs, where different groups perceive their interests as inherently opposed, hindering cooperation and understanding.

2. Weakening of Social Cohesion: Disenfranchisement efforts send a message of exclusion, signaling to affected communities that their voices and concerns are not valued in the democratic process. This can result in a breakdown of social cohesion and a weakened sense of belonging to the larger societal fabric.

3. Erosion of Trust Between Communities: When certain groups are systematically disenfranchised, it can breed mistrust between communities. Those affected may view the actions of those in power as discriminatory, while others may perceive calls for inclusivity as a threat to their own interests. This mutual suspicion can exacerbate social tensions.

4. Increased Political Polarization: Disenfranchisement efforts can contribute to political polarization, wherein individuals and groups become more ideologically extreme and less willing to find common ground. This hampers constructive dialogue and compromises necessary for effective governance.

5. Undermining Social Progress: Divisions caused by disenfranchisement can impede social progress by diverting attention from critical issues that require collective efforts. Rather than focusing on common challenges, society may become consumed by internal conflicts.

6. Hampering Efforts for Equality and Justice: Disenfranchisement based on race or gender perpetuates systemic inequalities and social injustices. It reinforces discriminatory practices and hinders progress towards building a more inclusive and just society.

7. Impact on Democratic Participation: When individuals feel excluded from the democratic process, voter turnout and political participation may decline. People may feel disillusioned and disengaged, further diminishing the democratic system's ability to represent the diverse voices within the population.

Addressing the polarization and division resulting from disenfranchisement requires confronting the root causes of discriminatory practices and actively promoting inclusivity and equality. Protecting voting rights for all citizens and working towards equitable representation in government are essential steps to mitigate divisions.

Fostering a culture of respect for diverse perspectives, promoting intergroup dialogue, and encouraging civic engagement are vital in bridging divides and building trust between communities. Moreover, acknowledging historical injustices and working towards redressing them can help heal social rifts and promote reconciliation.

Efforts should also focus on creating an environment that values shared identities and common goals while appreciating and celebrating the diversity that enriches society. By recognizing the strength that comes from unity in diversity, societies can move towards a more cohesive and harmonious future, fostering a sense of belonging and collective responsibility for the well-being of all citizens.

Ultimately, combating polarization and division requires a collective commitment to democratic principles that honor the rights and dignity of every individual. By building bridges of understanding and embracing a spirit of inclusion, societies can confront the challenges posed by disenfranchisement and strive for a more united and resilient future.

6. Impact on Representation: When certain groups are systematically denied voting rights, their voices and concerns are silenced. This can result in a lack of representation for these communities in government and policy-making processes.

Representation lies at the core of a functional and responsive democratic system. It is the principle that elected officials should reflect the diverse perspectives and interests of the entire population they serve. When voting rights are denied to specific groups, it creates a significant imbalance in representation, leading to underrepresentation or even complete exclusion of these communities from the decision-making processes that shape their lives.

1. Silencing of Voices: Denying voting rights effectively silences the voices of the affected communities. It denies them a platform through which they can articulate their needs, aspirations, and concerns, leaving them without a say in the issues that directly impact their well-being

and future.

2. Lack of Inclusive Policies: When underrepresented communities are excluded from the policy-making process, their unique experiences and challenges are often overlooked. This lack of representation can lead to the formulation of policies that do not adequately address the needs of these marginalized groups, perpetuating existing inequalities.

3. Reinforcing Social Inequities: The denial of voting rights can exacerbate social inequities. Policies and laws that adversely affect certain communities may go unchallenged, leading to a reinforcing cycle of disadvantage and discrimination.

4. Weakening of Democratic Legitimacy: A lack of representation undermines the legitimacy of the democratic system itself. When citizens feel their voices are not heard and their interests are not considered, it erodes trust in elected officials and the democratic process.

5. Missed Opportunities for Social Progress: Underrepresented communities often have unique insights into addressing social issues and advancing societal progress. Denying their participation in decision-making deprives society of valuable

perspectives and innovative solutions.

6. Disengagement from Civic Life: When communities are denied representation, they may become disenchanted with the political process and disengage from civic life. This disengagement can lead to reduced voter turnout and a decline in political participation.

7. Weakening of Social Cohesion: A lack of representation can deepen social divisions and reinforce feelings of exclusion and alienation. This can weaken social cohesion and create barriers to building a sense of collective identity and shared goals.

To address the impact on representation, it is imperative to protect voting rights for all citizens and actively work to dismantle barriers that prevent equal access to the democratic process. Efforts to combat voter suppression, promote voter registration, and expand early voting options can enhance democratic participation and representation.

Moreover, fostering a culture of inclusivity and diversity in politics is crucial for promoting representation that truly reflects the richness of society. Encouraging underrepresented groups to participate in political processes, supporting diverse candidates, and actively listening to the concerns of marginalized communities can create a more inclusive political landscape.

Political leaders and institutions play a pivotal role in ensuring that all citizens' voices are heard and respected. By prioritizing policies that address the needs of marginalized groups, advocating for social justice, and actively seeking input from underrepresented communities, elected officials can foster a more inclusive and responsive governance.

Ultimately, strengthening representation is not only about achieving fair political participation but also about building a more equitable and just society. By actively working towards inclusive representation, societies can move closer to realizing the democratic ideal of governance that truly reflects the interests, concerns, and aspirations of all its citizens, irrespective of their background or identity.

8. Challenges to Equal Opportunity: Equal opportunity is a key democratic ideal. Stripping away voting rights can exacerbate existing inequalities, hindering progress toward a more just and equitable society.

Quality opportunity lies at the heart of democratic values. It asserts that every individual should have an equal chance to succeed and thrive, regardless of their background or circumstances. Voting rights are not only essential for political representation but also serve as a gateway to equal opportunity. When these rights are denied or suppressed, it can have profound implications for social mobility, access to resources, and the overall trajectory of individuals' lives.

1. Perpetuating Historical Injustices: Denying voting rights to specific groups perpetuates historical injustices. Many marginalized communities, such as black people, people of color, and women, have faced a long history of discrimination and disenfranchisement. Stripping away their voting rights rekindles the legacy of oppression and reinforces systemic inequalities that have persisted for generations.

2. Reinforcing Social and Economic Disparities: Equal opportunity is predicated on leveling the playing field, but voter disenfranchisement tilts the balance further in favor of those in power. Policies that favor specific interests can be perpetuated, reinforcing social and economic disparities that hinder upward mobility and fair access to opportunities.

3. Impact on Education and Employment: Equal opportunity in education and employment is deeply connected to democratic principles. When certain communities are systematically excluded from the democratic process, they may face barriers to accessing quality education and employment opportunities, hindering their prospects for social and economic advancement.

4. Impeding Social Progress: Stripping away voting rights limits the ability of marginalized communities to

advocate for progressive policies that promote social justice, civil rights, and economic equality. Progress toward a more just and equitable society is impeded when voices from underrepresented groups are silenced.

5. Diminishing Social Cohesion: Equal opportunity fosters a sense of shared identity and mutual responsibility for the well-being of all citizens. However, when voting rights are denied to specific groups, it fosters divisions, undermines social cohesion, and erodes the sense of collective responsibility for societal progress.

6. Weakening Democratic Legitimacy: A democracy's legitimacy rests on the principle of representing the will of the people. Denying voting rights can undermine the legitimacy of elected officials and weaken trust in democratic institutions. This, in turn, can lead to a decline in civic engagement and a sense of alienation from the political process.

7. Hindering Policy Solutions: Equal opportunity requires responsive and inclusive policy solutions. Disenfranchisement limits the representation of affected communities, making it challenging to address issues that disproportionately impact marginalized groups effectively.

To overcome challenges to equal opportunity, societies must prioritize the protection and promotion of voting rights for all citizens. Efforts to combat voter suppression, expand voting access, and dismantle discriminatory practices are essential steps in advancing democratic values and ensuring equal opportunity.

Moreover, investing in education, healthcare, and economic policies that promote social mobility and equality are crucial for leveling the playing field. Providing marginalized communities with the resources and opportunities necessary to fully participate in civic life and pursue their aspirations can help bridge the gaps created by voter disenfranchisement.

By upholding the democratic ideals of equal opportunity, inclusivity, and representation, societies can move towards building a more equitable and just future. It requires a collective commitment to dismantling systemic barriers, embracing diversity, and actively working towards a society where every individual's voice is heard and valued. Only through such concerted efforts can democracy realize its true potential as a force for positive change and progress.

8. Potential for Authoritarianism: Suppression of voting rights can pave the way for authoritarianism. When certain groups are denied the right to vote, it weakens the checks and balances that are crucial for safeguarding

democratic governance.

Authoritarianism thrives on concentrating power in the hands of a few, often at the expense of the broader population's rights and freedoms. When voting rights are suppressed, it opens the door for those in power to manipulate the democratic process, consolidate authority, and undermine the essential checks and balances that ensure accountability and transparency.

1. Weakening of Democratic Institutions: Voting rights serve as a foundational pillar of democratic governance. When specific groups are denied the right to vote, the legitimacy of democratic institutions may come under question. This can lead to a decline in public trust and create a void of confidence in the ability of democratic systems to function effectively.

2. Erosion of Separation of Powers: In a functioning democracy, the separation of powers between the executive, legislative, and judicial branches act as a safeguard against unchecked authority. Suppression of voting rights can disrupt this balance, as the ruling authorities may exert undue influence over the other branches, leading to an erosion of democratic checks and balances.

3. Threat to Free and Fair Elections: The right to vote is

foundational to ensuring free and fair elections. When certain groups are systematically disenfranchised, it opens the door for election manipulation, gerrymandering, and other forms of electoral interference, all of which undermine the integrity of the democratic process.

4. Silencing Dissent and Minority Voices: By suppressing voting rights, authoritarian forces seek to silence dissenting voices and marginalize minority perspectives. This stifling of diverse opinions weakens the richness of democratic discourse and hampers the ability to find balanced and inclusive policy solutions.

5. Expansion of Executive Powers: The denial of voting rights can lead to the concentration of power in the executive branch of government. Without robust representation, the executive may accumulate more authority, leading to a breakdown in the system of checks and balances that are essential for democratic governance.

6. Increased Vulnerability to Corruption: Authoritarian regimes are often characterized by corruption and lack of accountability. When certain groups are denied the right to vote, it can exacerbate corruption by diminishing the mechanisms that would otherwise hold elected officials accountable to the interests of all citizens.

7. Polarization and Divisiveness: Authoritarian forces may exploit divisions and exploit the suppression of voting rights to perpetuate social polarization. By pitting different groups against each other, these regimes can further consolidate their power while undermining the sense of national unity.

To safeguard against the potential for authoritarianism, it is crucial to protect and promote voting rights for all citizens, irrespective of their background or identity. Strong democratic institutions, robust independent media, an active civil society, and a culture of democratic norms are essential for upholding the principles of accountability, transparency, and inclusivity.

Efforts to combat voter suppression, strengthen electoral integrity, and promote political education are vital steps in fortifying democratic resilience. Encouraging the active participation of all citizens in civic life, promoting dialogue, and fostering a commitment to democratic values are crucial in preserving the democratic system's integrity.

Ultimately, protecting voting rights is not merely a matter of political inclusion; it is about preserving the essence of democracy itself. By standing firm against attempts to suppress voting rights and embracing the principles of democratic governance, societies can shield themselves from the dangers of authoritarianism and move towards a more just, equitable, and democratic future.

9. Threat to Civil Rights Movement Gains: Disenfranchisement efforts can roll back the gains made through the civil rights movement and other historical struggles for human rights and equality.

The civil rights movement was a transformative and hard-fought struggle that sought to secure fundamental human rights and equality for marginalized communities, particularly black people and other people of color. It brought about significant legal and social changes, including the landmark Voting Rights Act of 1965, which aimed to protect the voting rights of racial minorities.

However, efforts to disenfranchise specific groups, particularly those that were the primary targets of the civil rights movement, pose a grave threat to the progress made during that pivotal era.

1. Erosion of Voting Rights Protections: The disenfranchisement efforts targeting racial minorities and other historically marginalized groups undermine the very protections put in place to safeguard their voting rights. These efforts effectively negate the progress made by the civil rights movement and diminish the impact of the Voting Rights Act.

2. Reversal of Inclusivity and Diversity Gains: The civil rights movement was a powerful advocate for inclusivity, diversity, and equal representation in

all facets of society. Disenfranchisement disrupts these advancements, potentially marginalizing these communities once again and hindering their progress toward greater representation and participation.

3. Undermining Social Justice and Equity: The civil rights movement aimed to rectify historical injustices and promote social justice and equity. Disenfranchisement efforts counteract these principles by perpetuating systemic discrimination and denying affected communities the ability to participate fully in the democratic process.

4. Threat to Intersectional Movements: The civil rights movement laid the groundwork for intersectional movements that seek to address overlapping forms of discrimination and oppression. Disenfranchisement affects the multiple layers of identity that individuals hold, potentially undermining the collective efforts of intersectional movements.

5. Disregard for Human Rights: Disenfranchisement not only weakens voting rights protections but also disregards the fundamental human rights that every individual is entitled to, irrespective of their race, gender, or background. Denying people, the right to vote infringes upon their dignity and self-determination.

Retreat from Inclusive Democracy: The civil rights movement sought to expand the concept of democracy to be more inclusive and representative of all citizens. Disenfranchisement represents a retreat from this inclusive vision, limiting democratic participation and undermining the principles of equal citizenship.

To safeguard the gains made by the civil rights movement and other historical struggles for human rights and equality, it is essential to protect voting rights as a cornerstone of democracy. This requires addressing voter suppression tactics, promoting voter education and registration, and combating discriminatory practices that hinder access to the ballot box.

Moreover, continuing to advocate for social justice, inclusivity, and equal representation is crucial in advancing the principles that underpin the civil rights movement. By recognizing the interconnectedness of various struggles for justice, societies can work towards building a more equitable and inclusive future for all citizens.

By actively opposing disenfranchisement and embracing the legacy of the civil rights movement, societies can reinforce their commitment to human rights, equality, and democracy. By preserving and building upon the gains made through historical struggles, we can move towards a more just, inclusive, and democratic society for present and future generations.

10. Long-Term Impact on Democracy: If not addressed, the denial of voting and human rights to certain groups can have long-term consequences for democracy. It can create a system that perpetuates discrimination and inequality, threatening the very foundation of democratic governance.

The denial of voting and human rights to specific groups is not merely a short-term setback; it can have far-reaching implications for the functioning and health of a democratic society. When certain communities are systematically excluded from the democratic process, it creates a cycle of discrimination, perpetuating social inequalities and undermining the principles that uphold democracy.

1. Reinforcement of Structural Discrimination: Denying voting and human rights reinforces structural discrimination within society. By systematically excluding certain groups, it sustains the systemic barriers that prevent equal access to opportunities, resources, and representation.

2. Diminishing Trust in Democratic Institutions: When citizens perceive that the democratic system does not represent their interests, it erodes trust in democratic institutions. This lack of trust can lead to disengagement

from civic life, decreased voter turnout, and a weakened belief in the efficacy of democratic processes.

3. Impact on Political Participation: The denial of voting rights can lead to reduced political participation, particularly among marginalized communities. As these communities are excluded from decision-making, they may feel disempowered and discouraged from engaging in the democratic process.

4. Strained Social Cohesion: Democracy relies on a sense of shared purpose and common identity. The denial of voting and human rights can create divisions and foster social fragmentation, weakening social cohesion and hindering collective action.

5. Entrenchment of Political Disparities: The exclusion of certain groups from voting and human rights can exacerbate political disparities. It can lead to policies that disproportionately favor specific interests, further deepening economic and social inequalities.

6. Undermining the Principle of Equal Citizenship: The foundation of democracy rests on the idea of equal citizenship, where every individual's voice and rights are valued equally. The denial of voting and human rights undermines this principle, distorting the concept of citizenship and creating a hierarchy of participation.

7. Threat to Democratic Stability: A democracy relies on the consent and participation of its citizens. The denial of voting and human rights can fuel social unrest and political instability, threatening the sustainability of the democratic system.

To address the long-term impact of the denial of voting and human rights, societies must prioritize the protection of these rights for all citizens. It requires active efforts to combat voter suppression, promote inclusive electoral practices, and dismantle discriminatory laws and practices.

Moreover, advancing social justice and equality is essential in ensuring that all members of society have an equal opportunity to participate in civic life and influence the decision-making processes that affect them.

Fostering a culture of democratic values, respect for human rights, and inclusivity is crucial for nurturing a healthy and vibrant democracy. By actively working to remove barriers to voting and human rights, societies can uphold the foundational principles of democratic governance and create an environment where all citizens can thrive, participate, and contribute to the collective well-being. Only through such sustained efforts can democracy truly fulfill its promise of representing and serving the interests of all its citizens, ensuring a more just, equitable, and resilient society for generations to come.

Addressing the threat to democracy posed by the denial of voting and human rights requires a commitment to uphold democratic principles and human rights. Promoting voter education, combating voter suppression, and protecting the voting rights of all citizens are essential steps in safeguarding democracy. Ensuring equal access to voting and representation for all communities, regardless of race, gender, or other characteristics, is crucial for fostering an inclusive and vibrant democracy. By actively opposing attempts to disenfranchise specific groups and advocating for equal rights and representation, society can work toward preserving the integrity and strength of dem ocratic governance.

CHAPTER 42
Conclusion Mastering The Power of Belief

In the pages of "Mastering the Power of Belief," we embarked on a profound journey through the intricacies of belief, exploring how it shapes our world, influences our actions, and defines the very essence of who we are as individuals and societies. From the interplay between perception and belief to the transformative impact of visionary leaders, we have unraveled the profound implications of our beliefs on personal, social, and global scales.

Throughout this exploration, we recognized that belief is not a mere abstract idea but a force that permeates every aspect of our lives. It shapes our attitudes, molds our behaviors, and guides our decisions. It holds the power to build bridges or construct walls, to inspire progress or perpetuate regression. As we traversed the landscape of belief, we discovered its pivotal role in shaping culture, politics, and societal norms, making it an indispensable subject for understanding human existence and potential

We delved into the sources of belief, recognizing the role of religion, spirituality, and scientific rationality as distinct avenues through which convictions are formed. The influence of authority figures, the power of conditioning, and the significance of emotional and intuitive beliefs emerged as critical factors in understanding the intricate mechanisms of belief formation.

Furthermore, we acknowledged the dual nature of belief as both a tool of empowerment and a potential source of adversity. It can serve as a profound coping mechanism in times of uncertainty and adversity, offering hope and comfort in challenging circumstances. However, it also has the capacity to propagate misinformation, perpetuate inequalities, and obstruct the path towards a better future.

We confronted the ominous implications when half of the country believes truth is a lie and a lie is truth. The erosion of trust, the rise of disinformation, and the polarization of society all serve as stark reminders of the fragility of democratic ideals and the necessity to uphold the principles of equality, inclusivity, and representation.

We witnessed the threat posed by the denial of voting and human rights to certain groups, which can erode the foundations of democracy, perpetuate discrimination, and undermine the progress achieved through the hard-fought struggles of historical movements for civil and human rights.

Yet, amidst the challenges and complexities, we found hope. We recognized that the power of belief is not a fixed or immutable force but one that can be harnessed and channeled towards positive transformation. We explored how questioning our beliefs and embracing critical thinking can lead to personal growth and societal evolution.

In the face of global challenges, we discovered that collective belief could drive efforts to address pressing issues like climate change and poverty, envisioning a future where the power of belief is channeled towards unity, compassion, and progress.

As we conclude this journey, we are reminded that belief is not solely a subject of academic inquiry but a force that demands conscious reflection and ethical responsibility. It is a call to action for each individual to introspect, question, and challenge their own convictions to build a more enlightened and compassionate world.

May the insights gained from "Mastering the Power of Belief" inspire us to bridge divides, dismantle barriers, and cultivate beliefs that empower rather than oppress. Let us harness the power of belief to chart a course towards a future that celebrates our shared humanity, embraces diversity, and upholds the principles that lie at the heart of a thriving democracy.

Together, as we master the power of belief, we have the potential to shape a world where thruth triumphs over falsehoods, justice overcomes inequities, and the indomitable spirit of humanity prevails, propelling us towards a future where belief serves as a catalyst for progress, compassion, and collective well-being.

With this understanding, we embark on a new chapter in our shared journey, armed with the wisdom and insights gained from "Mastering the Power of Belief," ready to meet the challenges of tomorrow with renewed determination and unwavering belief in the possibility of a better world.

Peace and blessings to all my family, the world over, friends and readers, power, NO DOUBT!

"*NOW BELIEVE*"

WHATEVER YOUR MIND

CAN CONCEIVE

AND BELIEVE

IT CAN ACHIEVE!

ABOUT THE AUTHOR

I AM a pastor, I AM a teacher, I AM a writer, I AM an author, I AM a photographer I AM an entrepreneur, and I AM the oldest son of eight siblings and sharecropper parents. I AM God's man, chosen by God at birth and set apart for times such as this to do His will. I AM who God, says I AM, and I AM, the master of my own belief system.

I was born in a segregated mill village in Pacolet Mills, S.C. 79 years ago. I AM the author of 21 books.

Dr. Davis M Byars Jr

Pastor Ebenezer Baptist Church

487 Dicks Hill Parkway

Mt. Airy, Georgia 30563 Phone: 706-778-5710

e-mail: pastordavisebc@gmail.com

NOTES

NOTES